One Nation, Many Peoples
Immigration in the United States

~ A Resource Book ~

Produced by Knowledge Unlimited®, Inc.
PO Box 52, Madison, WI 53701-0052
(800)356-2303 or (608)836-6660

ISBN 1-55933-200-X

One Nation, Many Peoples

Immigration in the United States

A Resource Book

by Julia Pferdehirt and the staff of Knowledge Unlimited, including Dave Schreiner, Liza DiPrima, Ann Kniskern.

Knowledge Unlimited®, Inc., wishes to thank the following people for their help in compiling primary sources and other material for *One Nation, Many Peoples*: Heidi Alvarez, Seeta Chaganti, Matt Cibula, Lester J. D'Costa, Joan Donnelly, Dadisi Elliott, Linda Endsley, Nelson Gabriel, Eitan and Sharon Geva, Molly Laitman, Rosie Truong, Bobson Wong, and the Crossroads School, New York City.

ISBN 1-55933-200-X

Table of Contents

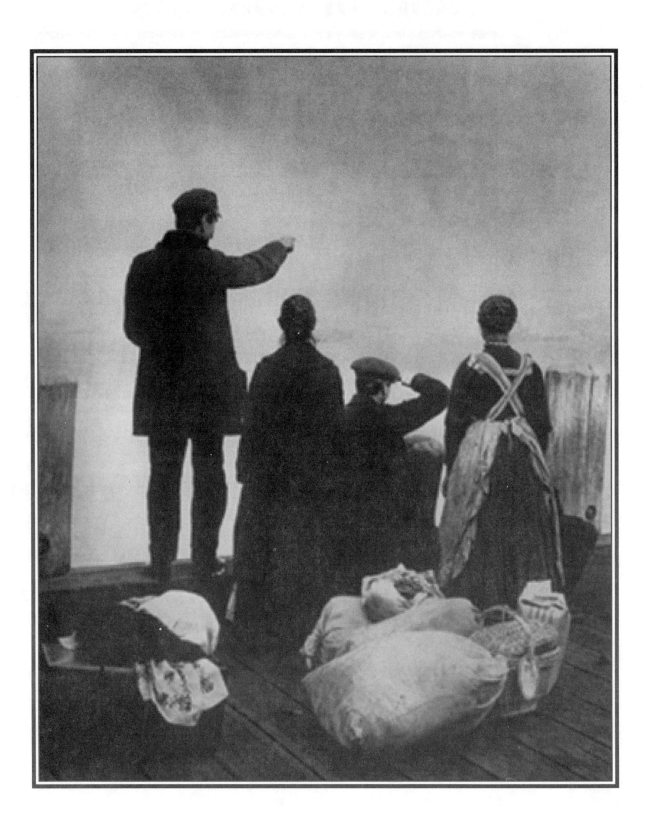

One Nation, Many Peoples

ONE NATION, MANY PEOPLES will introduce your students to the lives, experiences, and contributions of immigrants in American life and history. From the Chinese laborers whose skill and industry helped build our nation's railroads to the diverse Spanish-speaking groups that have left indelible imprints on American language, foods, and music, immigrants have shaped life and culture in the United States.

Truly multicultural education recognizes contributions and influences from all sources. The impacts of uniquely Native American or African American cultures and traditions have been explored in recent years. But those are pieces of a larger puzzle that must be explored as well.

It has become increasingly apparent that the "melting pot" image that was once held up as the model of America was never accurate. Immigrants have never dissolved into a cultural purée; groups have kept traditions, music, folkways, foods, and a sense of ethnic identity. At the same time, immigrants have become Americans. Their beloved and valuable ethnic inheritances have not disappeared, they have evolved to include new neighbors, a new language, and a shared culture of diversity. The "melting pot" is really a collage or a mosaic of overlapping, unique, multicolored images that create a single picture when viewed from a distance.

ONE NATION, MANY PEOPLES includes a wealth of information, teaching ideas, and projects to help you teach your students about many of the immigrant groups that have come to this country. This book is divided into eight units, corresponding to eight geographic regions: **East Asia, Southeast Asia, South Asia and the Middle East, Eastern Europe, Western Europe, West Africa, Mexico and Central America,** and **the Caribbean.** The book is designed to be flexible: You can use the materials provided here to teach only one unit, all eight, or any combination in between, based on your own curriculum and teaching needs. Included here are some suggestions and hints to help you get the most out of this book.

At the front of this book, you will find reproducible Project Sheet masters for individual and group projects. These include a **Timeline, Journey Map, History Mystery Scavenger Hunt,** and **In the News Today.** These projects may be used with any single unit or with all eight units. You can repeat any or all of them as you study different regions of the world. Or you can combine different regions of the world in a single project (a single Timeline or Journey Map, for example) for an interesting comparison of different immigrant groups.

In addition to these general projects, each of the eight units also contains information, report topics, and project ideas specific to that immigrant group. Each unit opens with a section of teacher instructions, followed by pages that are written for your students and may be duplicated at your discretion for their use:

- ❦ **Why They Came to America** is a historical summary about the featured group.

- ❦ **In Their Own Words** includes primary source materials from and about that group.

- ❦ **We Change — Traditions Remain** explains the history and meanings behind some of the cultural traditions of the featured group.

- ❦ **Folkways in a Nation of Immigrants** is a list of suggested hands-on projects and crafts designed to expose your students to the folkways, traditions, and culture of the immigrant group they are studying. Craft instructions and recipes are also included.

- ❦ And a list of **Research and Writing Topics** specific to each unit will help students tailor their report topics and research. Each Research and Writing Topics list starts off with projects appropriate for younger students or those with limited reading skills.

Folkways and Research and Writing projects may be done individually or in groups. Research and Writing ideas often include suggestions for an oral presentation to the class. You can decide whether oral presentations are necessary or desirable. Folkways projects may lend themselves to a period- or day-long "International Day" when students share everything from food to dioramas to traditional crafts.

Each unit includes teacher suggestions for class enrichment activities. Inviting speakers, viewing films, or listening to traditional music will broaden students' understanding of the cultures and traditions brought by immigrants to this country. These experiences will increase students' appreciation for those diverse cultures, heritages, and traditions.

At the back of this book, you will find a **Resource List** containing a partial list of recommended fiction and nonfiction books, as well as articles, films, and other sources for students to gather information and learn more about the groups you are studying. The list is broken into eight sections, corresponding to the eight study units.

The lessons and information in this book will help students learn about the history and experiences of American immigrants from eight regions around the globe. They will learn why people left their homelands and where, when, and how they carved out new lives for themselves in the U.S. As they read, do research, and enjoy crafts, foods, and traditions from around the world, we hope that students will have fun and learn to appreciate the history and heritage of the collage we call America.

Sample Unit Plans

The lessons in this guide are designed to flex with teacher and class schedules and needs. A single unit may be touched upon in two to three days in one class. Another teacher may choose to spend five to six days or even schedule a two week study on a single unit. This section includes some suggested outlines and timetables. The schedules that follow are, of course, only suggestions. You may use and adapt the materials to meet your needs and the demands of your curriculum.

2-3 Day Unit

Completing a unit in two to four days requires an emphasis on cooperative learning and careful evaluation and selection of materials and assignments. These unit study materials contain many more ideas and project suggestions than can realistically be included in such a limited study. Pre-selection of age, grade, and interest-appropriate materials and projects will help short-term studies run smoothly.

To save time, teachers may limit options for the Research and Writing or Folkways in a Nation of Immigrants segments of the unit, or simply select and assign topics themselves. Use of cooperative learning groups will also make the most of limited time. Library and resource center staff should be notified of research topics before students begin their research so materials are ready and accessible.

Please note that the first Research and Writing project suggestions in each unit are appropriate for students with below-grade-level reading skills. Research and Writing projects may be assigned to students individually or in groups.

Sample Schedule　　**DAY 1** View the video *The Golden Door: Our Nation of Immigrants*. *Time: 25 minutes for video, 10 minutes for discussion.*

Research and writing ideas for such a limited unit might include:

- ❦ Asking students to research and present a report on the life and contributions of one famous person from the ethnic/immigrant community being studied.

- ❦ Asking students to bring in one photo, graphic, drawing, or other illustration of the folkways, clothing, houses, foods, and other traditions of the ethnic/immigrant community being studied. Students can also be asked to find out information about the photo or illustration and to write a caption to teach others what they learned. Display photos and other illustrations on a bulletin board.

- ❦ Asking students to research and write a brief report about one historical event or era of significance to the ethnic/immigrant group. Examples of events may be found in the Research and Writing topic lists included with each unit.

Sample Unit Plans

Assign Project Sheets individually or as cooperative group work. Project sheets include Journey Maps, Timeline, History Mystery Scavenger Hunt, and In the News Today.

DAY 2 Present historical summary, using materials included with unit. *Time: 20 minutes.*

Students complete library or resource/media center research for Research and Writing assignment or Project Sheets.

DAY 3 Enrichment activity chosen from Teacher's Pages in each unit. *Time: 25-30 minutes.*

Students share what was learned and discovered during their research for the Research and Writing or Project Sheet assignments. *Time: 25-30 minutes.*

3-4 Day Unit

Sample schedule

DAY 1 Introduce unit. Traditional food or taped music may be used to draw students into the subject. Present historical summary included with this unit. Use map or globe to determine the homeland of the immigrant group being studied. Divide students into cooperative learning groups, assigning a Project Sheet to each group. Some teachers may wish to cover the Journey Map as part of the history presentation. *Time: approximately 30 minutes.*

Allow students on-line and library time to research the answers to questions on Project Sheets. *Time: 30 minutes.*

DAY 2 Enrichment activity. View the video *The Golden Door: Our Nation of Immigrants*, read aloud from a picture or children's chapter book or magazine article from the Resource List, or listen to a guest speaker. *Time: 30-40 minutes.*

Students share Project Sheet findings with class. *Time: 10 minutes.*

Present Research and Writing project assignments. Adjourn to library or resource/media center for research. *Time: 15-20 minutes.*

DAY 3 Enrichment activity. Play music, sample food, read excerpts from primary source materials included in the unit, or bring in sample of traditional craft. *Time: 10 minutes.*

Library and resource center for research. *Time: 50 minutes.*

DAY 4 Research and writing projects due. Teachers may choose to allow time for either an enrichment activity or for students to give brief oral presentations of material learned from their projects. Summarize unit.

Sample Unit Plans

One Week-Plus Unit

This suggested schedule allows significant time for research and project development. Teachers may wish to assign both Research and Writing and Folkways projects. This may be accomplished by creating cooperative learning groups and assigning both projects to each group of two to four students. Should both projects be assigned, an additional day will be required for presentations.

DAY 1 **Friday,** prior to the week-long unit. View the video *The Golden Door: Our Nation of Immigrants. Time: 25 minutes. Discussion time: 5-10 minutes.*

Briefly summarize the study topic of this specific unit for students. Using the Journey Map as a reference, tell students when and from where the ethnic/immigrant group you are studying came to the United States. (For example: "We'll be studying about immigrants from Western Europe. The region includes these countries. We'll be doing research, having speakers, listening to music, etc. First, however, I'd like to see what you can find out on your own over the weekend.") *Time: 10-15 minutes.*

Assign History Mystery Scavenger Hunt to half the students and the Timeline to the other half. *Due Monday.*

DAY 2 **Monday.** Enrichment activity chosen from Teacher's Pages suggestions included in each unit. *Time: 15-20 minutes.*

Discuss student findings on History Mystery Scavenger Hunt and Timeline. *Time: 10 minutes.*

Pass out historical summary information included in this unit. Ask students to read materials, or review with students in lecture format. Discussion following. *Time: 25 minutes.*

Assign In the News Today. This short project can be done at home, in the public library, or after school in the library or resource/media center. *Time: 5 minutes.*

DAY 3 **Tuesday.** Discuss In the News Today findings. *Time: 15 minutes.*

Hand out assignment materials for Research and Writing projects (see note above about including Folkways project assignments). Present options, organize groups if cooperative learning model is used, and pass around sign-up sheet for students to note their project choices. *Time: 15 minutes.*

Begin research in library or resource/media center. NOTE: Please prepare library or media center staff by presenting assignment topics prior to class period. If staff is ready with materials for students, it will allow students to select and check out books and other resources and begin research. *Time: 15-20 minutes.*

Sample Unit Plans

DAY 4 **Wednesday.** Teacher-planned enrichment activity from Teacher's Pages suggestions. *Time: 15-20 minutes.*

Library or resource/media center research. *Time: 30-40 minutes.*

Hand out Project Check-Up List, due Thursday. (A sample check-up list is included in this section.)

DAY 5 **Thursday.** Teacher-planned enrichment activity from Teacher's Pages suggestions. *Time: 15-20 minutes.*

Library or resource/media center research. *Time: 30 minutes.*

Check on status of ongoing project work. This process will enable you to determine that students are progressing appropriately with ongoing assignments. Your students can keep track of their progress on the Project Check-Up List. *Time: 10 minutes.*

DAY 6 **Friday.** Library or resource/media center research, in class computer research, work on visual aids, hands-on Folkways projects, etc.

DAY 7 **Monday.** Research and Writing projects due.

Option 1: If students were assigned projects from the Folkways in a Nation of Immigrants segment of the unit, this day could be set aside as an "International Day" festival. Students may share oral presentations, foods, crafts, or folk art projects with the class.

Option 2: If only Research and Writing projects were assigned, written work may be collected and the unit ends here. Or time may be set aside for oral reports on their written projects.

Option 3: If only Research and Writing projects were assigned, a special speaker, film, or other enrichment activity from Teacher's Pages suggestions may be scheduled.

Two Week Unit

A single unit may be scheduled for two complete weeks. This more leisurely pace will allow more teacher-planned enrichment activities, time to read aloud a fiction title from unit resource lists, watch a feature-length video if available, or receive speakers or presentations from community members. Allowing two weeks for this unit will permit students to complete Research and Writing projects *and* projects from the Folkways in a Nation of Immigrants list individually or in groups.

This longer time span permits more in-depth study and project-linked discovery learning. The addition of teacher-planned enrichment activities will require additional instructor time, however. Team-teaching with other classes may enable you to spread the planning load and, thereby, include as many enrichment activities as possible.

Project Check-Up List

☐ **Research and Writing Topic is:** _____

_____

Due on:_____

☐ **Folkways in a Nation of Immigrants topic is:** _____

_____

Due on: _____

☐ **Reading completed?**

yes _____ no _____

How much yet to complete?_____

☐ **Notes completed?**

yes _____ no _____

How much yet to complete?_____

☐ **Props, craft or food items, or visual aids completed?**

yes _____ no _____ **What is left to complete?** _____

☐ **Written report completed?** yes _____ no _____

☐ **Oral report completed?** yes _____ no _____

☐ **What plan do you have to complete this project by the due date?** _____

_____

_____

_____

☐ **If working in a group, are all group members clear about areas of responsibility?** yes _____ no _____

If not, what plan do you have to communicate clearly about tasks and responsibilities? _____

_____

_____

☐ **What assistance or information do you need to complete this assignment on time?** _____

_____

Timeline

Project Sheets

This Timeline will help students place people and events in a larger historical context. In classes where more than one unit from ONE NATION, MANY PEOPLES is being studied, you may want your students to start a new timeline for each group you study. Or you may ask students to put all the information they collect on a single timeline. Students can color-code different ethnic/immigrant groups so they can see and compare when and why different groups came to America, and what was happening in the world when they came.

The blackline master for the timeline may be reproduced on heavy paper and assembled end-to-end for use by individual students. Or you may wish to enlarge the master to create a classroom timeline. The symbols may also be reproduced for individual student use or enlarged for use on a classroom timeline.

The included symbols mark significant historical events. They should be placed by students on the timeline at or near the dates of their occurrence. Students will develop a sense of the flow of history by understanding, for example, whether an immigrant group arrived in the U.S. before or after the Civil War, before or after the introduction of the automobile, or during the era of pioneering and homesteading. You and your students may also wish to create symbols for benchmarks of your own.

Timeline

Project Sheets

Each of the following symbols represents an important event in American or world history. Do some research in almanacs, encyclopedias, books, on-line, and in other sources to find out when each of these events took place. Then, place each of the symbols at the correct spot on your timeline. Now do some research on the immigrant group you are studying. Indicate the major time period or periods when the group came to America on your timeline. Depending on the group, you may have to include a range of years, or even several different time periods. If necessary, note when people from different countries in the group came. If you are studying more than one group, your teacher may ask you to put all the groups you are studying on the same timeline, so you can compare when different immigrants came.

When you have completed your timeline, write your answers to the following questions on a separate sheet of paper, or discuss these questions as a class:

1. **What do you notice about the time when the immigrant group you're studying came over?**

   _____

2. **What major events were taking place at or around the time this group came?**

   _____

3. **Do you think these events had any bearing on the reasons this group came? Why or why not?**

   _____

4. **Do you think these events influenced the experience that these immigrants had when they got to America? How?**

   _____

5. **Did all or most of the people from this group come over at one particular time, or did they come in different waves? What do you think the reasons for this are?**

   _____

6. **If you have included two or more groups on one timeline, what differences do you notice in when they came to America? What do you know about these groups that would explain these differences?**

   _____

Timeline

These icons symbolize significant events in history. They should be placed on the timeline at or near the dates of their occurrence. You may also wish to add events of your own.

Invention of the automobile

Boxer rebellion

Columbus

Withdrawal from Vietnam

George Washington is President

Homestead Act

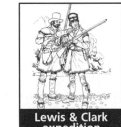
Lewis & Clark expedition

Abraham Lincoln is President

Charles Lindbergh's solo flight

Pilgrims land

Invention of the telephone

Pogroms

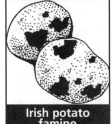
Irish potato famine

Prohibition

Railroad linked from east to west

The Great Depression

The first satellite, Sputnik

Gold discovered in California

Louisiana Purchase

NAFTA enacted

Revolutionary War

French Revolution

Revolution in Europe

Mexican War

Vietnam War

Civil War

World War One

World War Two

Korean War

Spanish-American War

TO PUT THE TIMELINE TOGETHER: Cut out Timeline segments along dotted lines. Match up letters on timeline ends (A to A, B to B, etc.). Tape or glue the ends together, overlapping them so that the dark strips on the ends of the sections are covered.

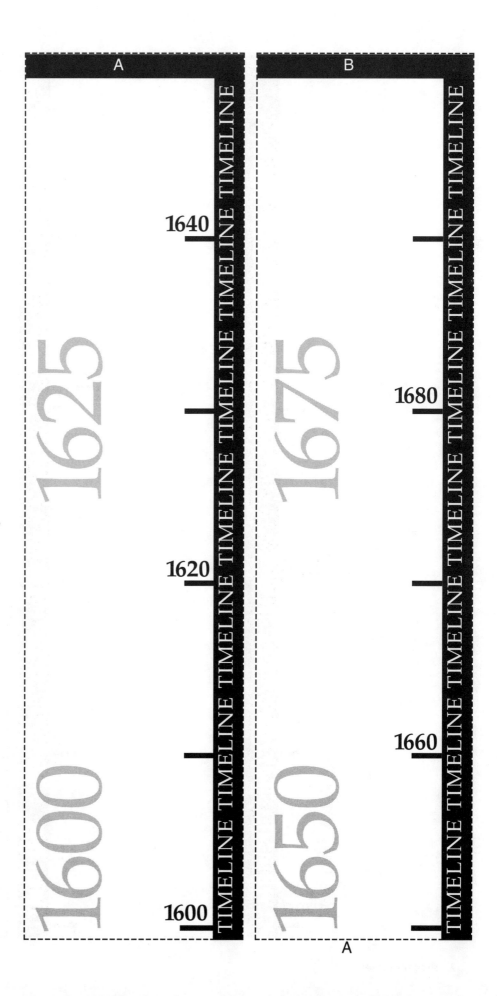

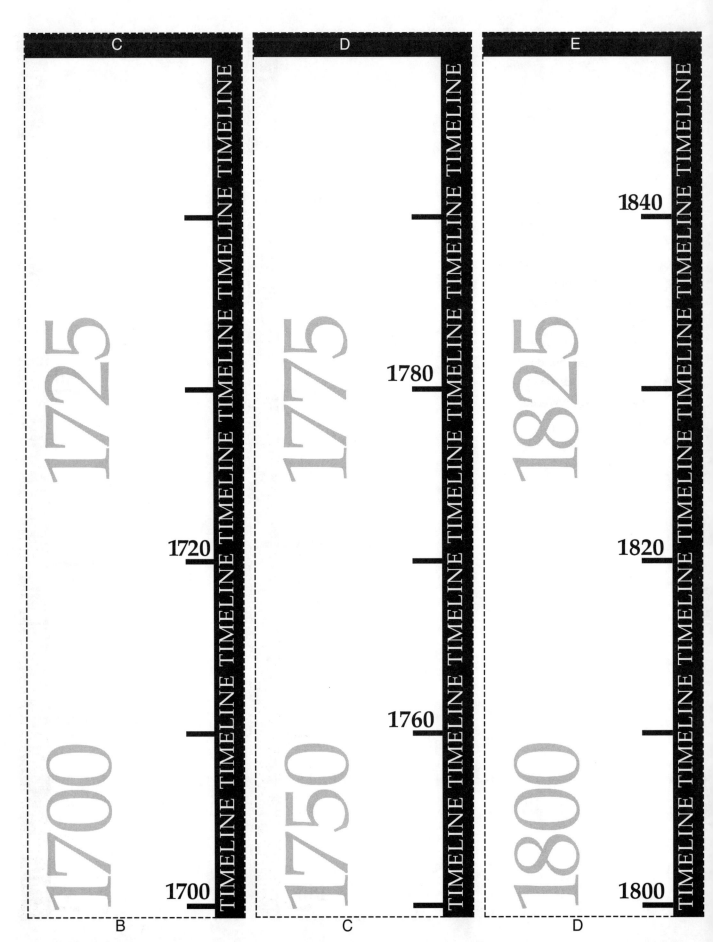

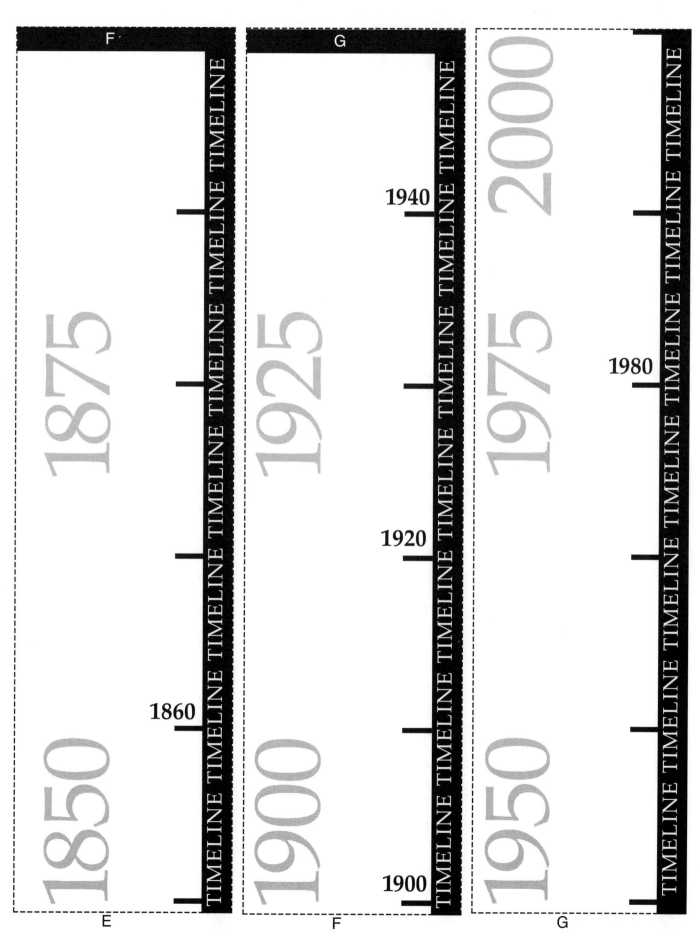

E

F

G

2000

1980

1975

1950

TIMELINE TIMELINE TIMELINE TIMELINE TIMELINE TIMELINE

1925

1940

1920

1900

1900

TIMELINE TIMELINE TIMELINE TIMELINE TIMELINE TIMELINE

1875

1860

1850

TIMELINE TIMELINE TIMELINE

F

G

Journey Map

Project Sheets

This project allows students to use library and reference materials to discover where each immigrant group came from, how they came, what route(s) they traveled, and where they eventually settled in the U.S. The Journey Maps are designed to be photocopied and passed out to individual students.

Instruct students to research the immigrant group or groups that you are studying. Then have them complete their Journey Maps. If you are studying more than one unit in this guide, you may want to have your students put all the groups on one map. If this is the case, instruct your students to color-code their maps, with a different color for each unit you are studying. Even if you are only studying immigrants from one area, you may suggest that students use different colors to represent different groups of immigrants from the same area of the world (for example, Chinese, Korean, and Japanese immigrants) to indicate how different people came and where they settled.

Students can include additional information about means of travel, destinations, and any unique or interesting qualities of settlement — such as the formation of ethnic enclaves in cities or the founding of towns and villages on the frontier — on the back of their Journey Map.

Two world maps are included here, to make it easier for students to show the routes immigrants took. One map places the U.S. in the West, for groups who traveled across the Atlantic Ocean from places like Europe. The other puts the U.S in the East, for those who traveled across the Pacific Ocean.

East

West

Project Sheets

Journey Map

Lots of people travel from place to place in airplanes or powerful, fast ships. To them, a three-hour delay is quite an inconvenience. But many immigrants had a very different experience coming to the U.S. For some, the journey to America took weeks or months. Some braved dangerous conditions and leaky, crowded ships just to reach Ellis Island or the San Francisco harbor. Once they arrived here, some journeyed through the U.S. in wagons on dirt roads, or squeezed into third-class passage on trains. Many families spent their life savings to send one member to America, then that person worked for years, saving every penny to buy passage for the rest of the family.

Show on this map where the immigrant group you are studying came from, what route(s) people used to travel to the U.S., and where they settled after arriving in America. This information is available at the library and in reference books, short histories, and through on-line sources.

If you are studying more than one immigrant group, or a group with people who settled in different areas, you can use different colors to show their different routes or destinations.

Two maps are included here. The Atlantic Route can be used for groups who came west to America, over the Atlantic Ocean. The Pacific Route is for groups who traveled east to America, across the Pacific Ocean. You can use either map for groups who came north or south.

After you are finished, answer the following questions. Include any other interesting information you find on the back of your Journey Map.

1. What mode or modes of transportation did the immigrant group use to get to America?

_____

2. How long did it take them to get here?

_____

3. Why did they take the route they did?

_____

4. Once they got to the U.S., why did they settle where they did?

_____

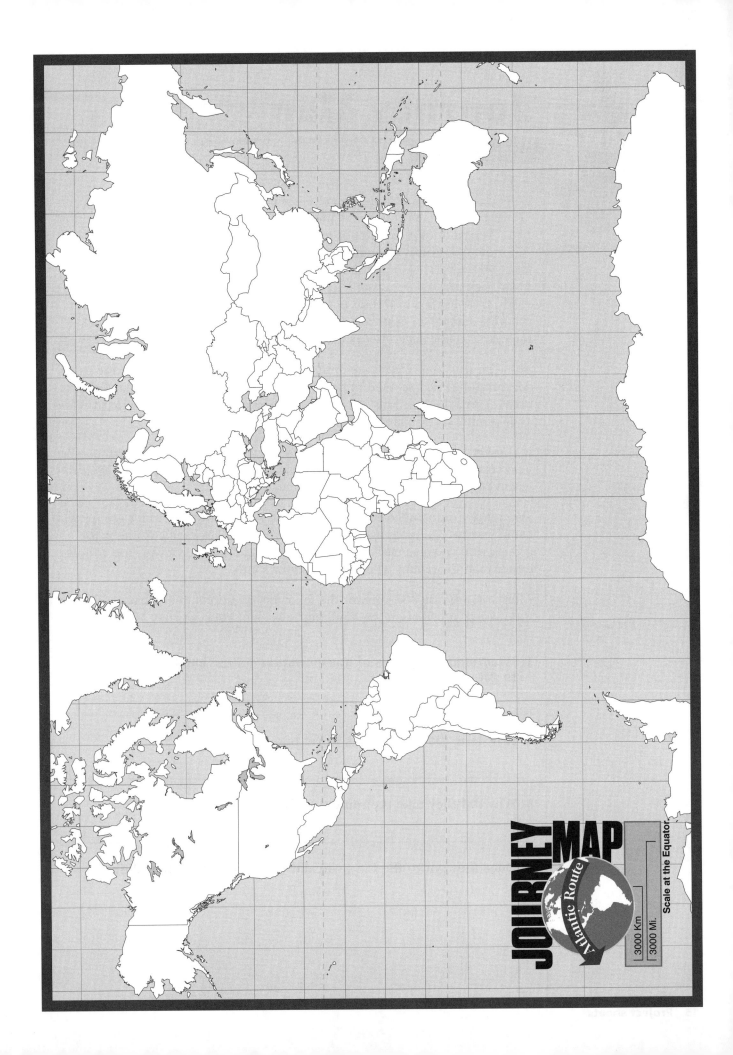

JOURNEY **MAP**

Atlantic Route

3000 Km
3000 Mi.

Scale at the Equator

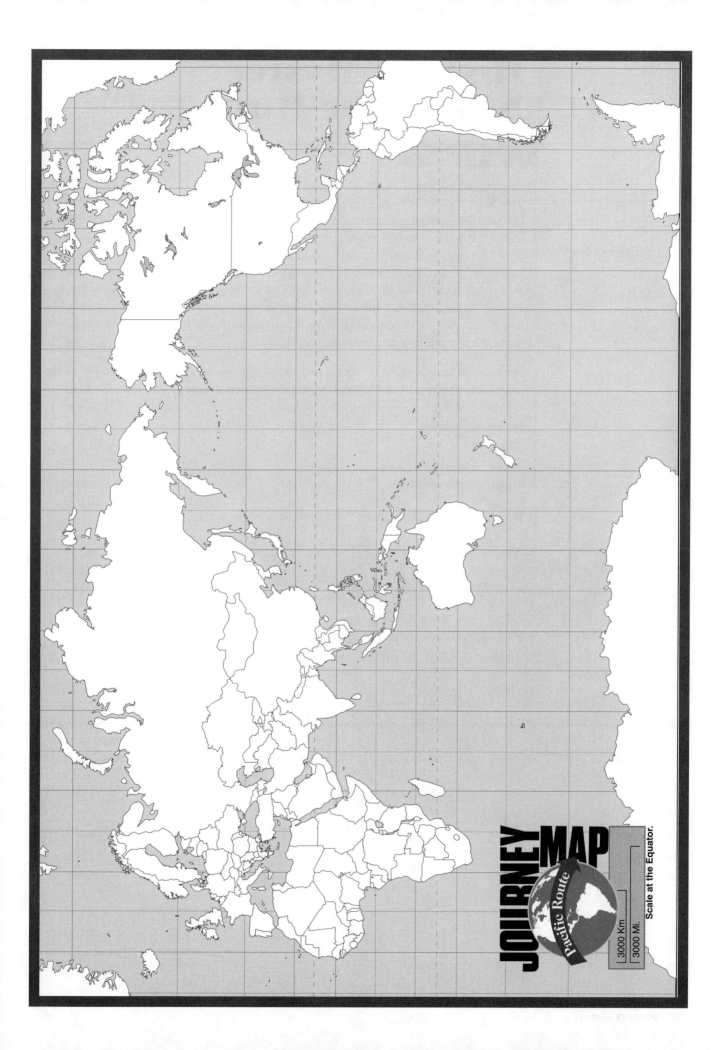

JOURNEY**MAP**

Pacific Route

3000 Km
3000 Mi.

Scale at the Equator.

History Mystery Scavenger Hunt

Project Sheets

The History Mystery Scavenger Hunt will help students understand what life was like when each immigrant group settled in the U.S. Students may benefit from researching these questions in groups and sharing answers with the entire class. You may choose to have different student groups do research on different groups of immigrants and answer all the questions. Or you may decide to split the questions up among the student groups. In any case, you may want to reserve some time for in-class discussion; it provides an opportunity to compare life today with the America immigrant groups came to during the last two centuries.

Student searches may be more productive if the library staff is aware of the project topics and your class's schedule before the project date. In addition, on-line services and computer research tools may provide helpful information for students.

Suggested schedule:

Divide students into groups of three to five.

Assign History Mystery Scavenger Hunt project.

Accompany students to library for research or send groups separately.

Allow time the following day or during a later period for students to share findings and compare the past and present.

History Mystery Scavenger Hunt

Immigrants came to America for many reasons. Some came to escape poverty, or because of religious or political persecution. War drove many people to leave their homes. Some were fortune-seekers. Some were refugees. Some were hungry and desperate. And some came here by force. They arrived in the United States hoping for opportunity and freedom. What kind of country did they find?

For the History Mystery Scavenger Hunt you will gather information about the era when the immigrant group you are studying came to America. The facts will show you a little about how Americans lived at that time. Knowing how people worked, played, voted, or earned money shows what kind of life immigrants found when they arrived here. Search the library and on-line reference materials to answer as many of these questions as you can. Use a separate sheet of paper if you need more room.

1. When did this group of immigrants come to America?

2. Were these immigrants welcome or not?

3. Who was the U.S. president?

4. Who was allowed to vote?

5. Name a discovery or invention that happened during that time.

6. How many people lived in the U.S.?

7. Was there a frontier at that time? If so, what was it?

8. What political events occurred then?

9. What military conflicts happened then?

10. What were the big world events?

11. If you were wealthy, how much money would you have made each year?

12. How much did a loaf of bread cost?

13. Name a famous author and/or book from the period.

14. If you took a cross-country trip, how would you have traveled?

15. Which territories were officially states at that time?

16. What were women's lives like?

17. What were children's lives like?

18. Can you find any political slogans from the time? What do they mean?

In the News Today

Project Sheets

In the News Today is a take-home research project designed to expose students to the present-day experience of members of the ethnic/immigrant group they are studying.

Students should use newspapers, magazines, and on-line services to find stories and news reports about the ethnic/immigrant group they're studying. They will share their findings with the class and discuss similarities and differences between the lives and experiences of people at the time they immigrated to America and their lives today.

Students may benefit if you require them to search for a variety of information. If some students search for stories and articles depicting life in the immigrant/ethnic group's homeland today, while others search for information about members of the group living in America, it may provide your class with a good comparison and an opportunity for further discussion.

You may wish to limit the time parameters for the articles and stories students may find, e.g., stories must be from the past 12-month period.

In the News Today

Project Sheets

News reporting today has helped make the world smaller. One hundred years ago, it took months for some Americans to hear the results of a presidential election. Today, if someone bungee jumps off the Brooklyn Bridge in the morning, the story will reach remote islands in Indonesia before dinnertime.

Immigrant groups that came to America have not disappeared. Ethnic traditions and history are still in the news today. Newspapers, magazines, and television shows cover political and social issues that are important to different groups. Events happen in the countries immigrants left to come to America.

Look in magazines, newspapers, and on television. An article about bilingual education involves Latino immigrants. A television special about World War Two tells a piece of the story of Jewish immigration. An article on Laos or Haiti may tell of wars or upheavals that could produce a new wave of immigrants from those countries today.

Find at least one story in any news medium about the immigrant group you are studying. The story may be about this ethnic group in America or about their homeland today. Or it may look back on the history of this immigrant or ethnic group.

Write a brief summary of the article, newscast, or television program. Explain why the topic is important and what information is given about the immigrant group you are studying. If possible, bring the story, or a copy, to class.

_____

_____

_____

_____

_____

_____

_____

_____

_____

Immigration: An Overview

For a long time now, the United States has taken in more immigrants and refugees than any other country in the world. The United States is, in fact, a nation of immigrants. Everyone in the United States came here from somewhere else. Our culture, our traditions, our language, and our history reflect this diverse and complex heritage.

Anthropologists believe the first migration took place thousands of years ago, when people from Asia, crossing a land bridge between what is now Russia and Alaska, came to this continent. By the time the first Europeans arrived in North America in the 15th century, the Americas were filled with people the Europeans called Indians. Beginning in the 1600s, immigration to the U.S. has taken place in four basic waves.

The first wave included the early colonists, most of whom came from England. Many others came from France, Germany, Ireland, Italy, Spain, and other countries in Europe. By the Revolutionary War, approximately 700,000 immigrants had arrived in the American colonies.

A large number of immigrants came here unwillingly from Africa as slaves. By 1807, when Congress made it illegal to import slaves, approximately 375,000 Africans had been brought here, most of them from West Africa.

The second wave of immigrants came here between 1820 and 1870. Almost eight million newcomers came to America in those years, most of them from Northern and Western Europe. About a third of the immigrants were Irish, fleeing a potato famine that struck Ireland in the 1840s. Another third were German, escaping political upheaval in their homeland. The discovery of gold in California and the building of the transcontinental railroad also brought many Asians, particularly Chinese immigrants, to this country.

The third wave, from 1880 to 1921, brought more than 23 million people to the United States. They came from almost every region of the world, but a majority came from Southern and Eastern Europe. This was the greatest sustained migration in history.

The fourth wave, from 1945 until the present, has come from Europe, Asia, Mexico, and the Caribbean Islands. The end of World War Two brought a number of European refugees to America. From the 1960s until the present, an estimated one million refugees from Cuba have fled Fidel Castro's regime for the U.S. In 1965, a new immigration act opened America's doors to people of nearly all lands. The 1965 act had a particular impact on Asian immigration. In the 1970s, refugees from Southeast Asia — Vietnam, Cambodia, and Laos — fled from the communist takeover of the region. Hundreds of thousands of immigrants from Southeast Asia have moved to this country. It is not known exactly how many Mexican immigrants there are in the U.S. Apart from the 95,000 Mexican nationals that immigrate legally to the U.S. each year, an estimated four million Mexicans are living in the U.S. without the government's permission.

Immigration: An Overview

Laws restricting immigration

Before 1875, there were no serious laws restricting immigration to the United States. In fact, during the mid-part of the 19th century, some states sent recruiters to Europe to attract settlers. But in the 1850s, the American, or Know-Nothing, Party campaigned against unrestricted immigration. In 1875, Congress passed a law that prohibited entry by convicts and prostitutes. In 1882, the Chinese Exclusion Law curbed Chinese immigration. Prior to that time, Chinese immigrants had come to the U.S. to mine for gold and help build the railroads across the nation. Congress extended the Chinese Exclusion Law in 1892 and then made it permanent in 1902. In 1907, the U.S. and Japanese governments entered into a so-called "gentleman's agreement." The Japanese agreed to discourage emigration, and the U.S. agreed to stop passing discriminatory immigration laws against Japanese people. This agreement was followed until 1924, when Congress barred the entry of all Asian laborers. Some historians believe this action fueled Japanese animosity to the U.S. before World War Two.

Congress passed several other laws in the 1920s that made it much harder for immigrants to come here. The National Origins Act of 1924 established immigration quotas for each country outside the Western Hemisphere. This law was followed by another that allowed a total of only about 150,000 immigrants a year to enter the United States from all countries in the world combined. Each nation's percentage of that 150,000 depended on the number of people from that country who were already in America.

In 1965, Congress passed a law that ended quotas for single nations. Instead, it set a limit of 120,000 immigrants from the Western Hemisphere and 170,000 from the Eastern Hemisphere, with no more than 20,000 from any one nation. Immigrants were admitted on a first-come, first-served basis, subject to a "preference system" that gave special standing to those with skills or abilities that were needed in the U.S., and those with relatives who were already here.

In the years since 1965, the United States has been open to people of all races, religions, and nations. Europe is no longer the main source of new-comers. Now, more than four out of every five immigrants are from Asia or Latin America.

In 1980, Congress passed a Refugee Act. This law allows in as many as 70,000 political refugees each year. A political refugee is defined as anyone who is unwilling to return to his or her home country because of "a well-founded fear of persecution."

In the mid 1980s, many lawmakers felt that new rules were needed to discourage illegal immigration. In 1986, a new law set up such rules. The Immigration Reform and Control Act of 1986 gave amnesty to an estimated three million illegal immigrants who had come here before 1982. However, it barred further illegal immigration and penalized employers who hired illegal immigrants.

Immigration: An Overview

Today, immigration continues to be a hot topic of debate in Congress and around the nation. About 800,000 immigrants are allowed into the country legally each year, and another 400,000 enter illegally. Many Americans think all immigration — legal and illegal — should be limited or even halted. Others favor proposals that would deprive illegal immigrants of social benefits, such as education or health care. Over the course of our nation's history, immigrants have been resented and feared by the people already in America. This pattern is likely to continue into the future — even as the United States remains a beacon of liberty to millions of potential immigrants around the world.

East Asia

This unit on East Asian immigrants focuses on the history, people, and cultures of China, Japan, and Korea.

The history of the immigrants who came here from these countries is marked by hostility and racism. The Chinese and Japanese who came here in the 19th and early 20th centuries faced harsh lives. They were sometimes the victims of mob violence, and were nearly always treated as second-class citizens. From 1882 to 1965, immigration from Asian countries was severely limited or banned altogether. During World War Two, 110,000 Japanese Americans were forced into camps on the West Coast, their property taken away from them and their lives shattered. Today, hostility still greets Asian immigrants, especially Korean immigrants in large cities.

Teachers may want to have their students study why Asian immigrants have faced racism. This is also a good place to study the various immigration laws that have been passed over the years. Many of these laws were aimed at curbing or stopping Asian immigration.

The following ideas would enhance and further develop this unit:

❧ Invite a Chinese, Japanese, or Korean member of your community to speak to the class.

❧ Ask students whose own ethnic background is Asian to interview their parents and grandparents about when, where, why, and how their families immigrated to the U.S.

❧ Bring in films or audio tapes to share music, dance, and drama from this region.

❧ Set aside a single time for students to share food, crafts, and projects from the We Change — Traditions Remain and Folkways in a Nation of Immigrants portions of the unit.

❧ Ask if any students of East Asian background have relatives who immigrated to the U.S. Invite them to tell the class about their experience as immigrants.

Why They Came to America

The following is a brief history of the people who came to the United States from East Asia — China, Japan, and Korea.

CHINA The earliest mass movement of Chinese immigrants to America happened in the middle of the 19th century. War and famine in the province of Canton led many Chinese men to leave their country for the "mountains of gold" in America. In 1848, gold was discovered in California, prompting a frantic "gold rush" in the United States. Thousands of people moved west to find riches. By the 1850s, gold fever had lured 20,000 Chinese men to San Francisco. They left China under contract to work for someone here, and with the understanding that they would return after their contracts expired. But many stayed on to work the gold fields for themselves. In addition, until about 1870, American businesspeople actively sought Chinese contract laborers — called "coolies." These laborers were instrumental in building the railroads that linked the eastern and western parts of the United States. At the same time, they were treated harshly. They had no rights as citizens and were sometimes treated almost as badly as slaves. By the early 1800s, nearly 500,000 Chinese immigrants were living on the mainland U.S. or in Hawaii. But in 1882, the U.S. government froze Chinese immigration with the Chinese Exclusion Act. Between 1882 and 1945, very few Chinese immigrants entered the United States legally. They and all other Asians living here were the victims of prejudice and fear. Asians were called a "Yellow Peril" who would take away jobs from white Americans. After World War Two, the ban on Chinese immigration was loosened because China had been allied with the U.S. in the war. In 1965, the immigration laws were loosened again, and ever since then, approximately 25,000 Chinese immigrants have arrived here each year.

At the present time, there are more than 1.5 million people of Chinese ancestry in America. Many Chinese immigrants live in urban centers like San Francisco, New York, Los Angeles, Chicago, and Honolulu, Hawaii. The "Chinatowns" in San Francisco and New York began as bachelor settlements because no Chinese women were allowed over as part of the first labor contracts. Instead, if a Chinese immigrant wanted to get married, he had to travel back to China to find a wife. After 1888, the U.S. outlawed this practice, stating that if Chinese men returned to China, they would have to stay there. Consequently, for a long time the ratio of Chinese men to women in this country was 19 to 1.

JAPAN Closing the door to Chinese immigration opened the door to Japanese immigration. The Chinese Exclusion Act was passed during a time when farms in California and plantations in Hawaii were rapidly expanding. Soon after the act was passed in 1882, employers discovered that there was a shortage of laborers for planting and harvesting crops. In 1886, the Emperor of Japan lifted a ban on emigration and between that year and 1924, about 380,000 Japanese came to America. About 200,000 of these immigrants settled in Hawaii and 180,000 went to the U.S. mainland — mostly to the West Coast. Nearly all of them became farmers, gardeners, or fruit and vegetable sellers because they were kept out of other occupations by whites. These first-generation Japanese immigrants were called

Why They Came to America

Issei. Unlike the Chinese, Japanese women were allowed to immigrate. And the Japanese used a system of arranged marriages — called the "picture bride" system — that allowed many Japanese women to join single Japanese men in this country. In 1907, Japan and the United States decided on what was called a "gentleman's agreement." The U.S. agreed not to pass laws barring immigrants from Japan, and the Japanese emperor agreed in return to stop much of the emigration to America. This agreement slowed the immigrant flow from Japan, especially to the West Coast.

Then in 1924, a new law prohibited all immigration from Asia. By this time, however, the Japanese people already here had begun families. Second-generation Japanese — called *Nisei* — were American citizens. But they were still the objects of racism and prejudice. They could not find jobs in the white world, and were kept out of most businesses. Instead they worked as farmers and landscape gardeners, and they owned businesses that served other Japanese Americans. In 1941, Japan's navy attacked the U.S. military installations at Pearl Harbor, Hawaii. The U.S.'s entry into World War Two made life even harder for Japanese Americans. On the West Coast, more than 110,000 Japanese Americans were forced out of their homes and away from their businesses. Their property was taken from them and they were herded into prison-like internment camps. They were imprisoned not because they had betrayed the U.S., but because many people *thought* they would. Although Japanese Americans fought bravely in the U.S. Army during the war, many of the soldiers' relatives lived in internment camps from 1942 to 1945. No plans were made to put Italian or German Americans into camps, even though the U.S. was also fighting Germany and Italy.

The 1965 Immigration Act, which lifted barriers to Asian immigration, brought many new Japanese immigrants to America. Today there are an estimated 845,000 people of Japanese ancestry living in this country. The majority of them still live in Hawaii and on the West Coast.

KOREA Koreans first came to U.S. territory in 1903, when they were recruited to work on sugar cane and pineapple plantations in Hawaii. Many of these workers left Korea to escape poverty and the takeover of their country by Japan. There were very few Koreans in the U.S. until after 1950, when communist North Korea invaded South Korea. The U.S. was part of a United Nations force that fought against North Korea from 1950 to 1953. After the war, about 5,000 South Korean women came to this country as the wives of American servicemen. The Immigration Act of 1965 brought many more South Koreans here. They came to escape poverty, the continuing threat of war with North Korea, and the often-repressive governments in their own nation.

There are an estimated one million people of Korean ancestry living in the United States today. Most of them live in large urban centers such as New York, Los Angeles, Philadelphia, and El Paso, Texas. Many of the immigrants are business and technical professionals. But many others own small shops, such

Why They Came to America

as grocery stores and restaurants, often in the poorest neighborhoods of a city. New Korean immigrants work together to improve their shops and move on to better locations. Korean immigrants have had to deal with hostility in their new country. The most visible portion of the Korean immigrant group — those who own grocery and other stores — have faced bitter accusations that they take from their local communities and give nothing in return. Korean Americans have been victimized by both hostile blacks and whites. There have been well-documented confrontations stemming from cultural clashes and accusations of prejudice on both sides. But Koreans still immigrate to the U.S. in search of what one immigrant calls "liberty, freedom, and security."

In Their Own Words

NOTE TO TEACHERS:

In this section, immigrants to the U.S. tell about their experiences coming to and living in America.

The first document is an excerpt from a magazine article published in 1909, where a white writer addresses the issue of Japanese immigration.

After reading the article, you might discuss issues of immigration, racism, and the idea of "amalgamation" with your class. This article may also provoke strong feelings about the writer's attitudes and prejudices. You may want to use the feelings and opinions your students express as a springboard for discussion. To what extent do the attitudes toward other races in the article reflect common attitudes of the time? To what extent do those attitudes exist today? What parallels can be drawn between attitudes toward immigration then and immigration today? What differences?

The other excerpt is of some poems written by hopeful Chinese immigrants in the 19th and early 20th centuries. The poems were written on Angel Island, in San Francisco Bay, where Chinese men were detained when they immigrated to the U.S. The men were kept on Angel Island until it was proven that they already had relatives in the United States, and that they had no communicable diseases.

You and your class may wish to analyze these poems and the context in which they were written. How must these men have felt as they waited on Angel Island? What do you think their expectations were as they embarked on their new lives in America? What do these poems tell you about the lives they left behind?

A White Californian's View on Japanese Immigration

This article by Chester H. Rowell, the editor of the Fresno, California, _Republican_, was written in 1909. It reflects the view held by many Californians in the early 1900s that Japanese immigration endangered white America.

Nothing can keep our Pacific Coast essentially a white man's country except our continued determination to keep it so. Nothing can preserve the essentially American social texture of the States bordering the Pacific except the preservation of the racial integrity of their population. And if that is not guarded, nothing can prevent the caste system and the wreck of free institutions from spreading backward over the mountains and across the plains, absolutely without limit, until the white man at last takes another stand. ... It is a question on which a blunder, once made, can never be rectified. The frontier of the white man's world must be established some day, somewhere. ... The problem is ours in the next few years, in California, Washington, and Oregon, and in the Capitol and White House. The consequences are the whole world's, everywhere, forever. ...

We ought to know by this time what immigration means, when once it starts. Ireland found us out, and moved over bodily. ... Northwestern Europe found us out, and all its surplus population moved over. Southern Italy found us out, and the surplus population of Naples and Sicily now digs our ditches and paves our streets. Southeastern Europe is finding us out, and the whole surplus population is moving over. ...

Asia has found us out too, and the flood from the Orient has started. Nothing can stop it unless we do. ... Literally hundreds of millions of brown men, yellow men, and bronze men would now like to come to America, for the same reasons that the Europeans wanted to come; and they will come, just as the Europeans have come, if they are equally free to do so. And then — the deluge!

The worst of it is that, temporarily and economically, we need them, and therefore some of our short-sighted capitalists desire them. It is a fair and empty land that awaits development, and it is capable of being exploited far more rapidly than the white man alone can do it. ...

Up to the present time the Japanese have refused to understand ... that insistence on race separation does not mean the assertion of race inferiority. Many of the Europeans whom we welcome are our inferiors. The Japanese, to whom we object, are, as a race, our equals. But they are a different race physically, and nature will keep them different through all the generations, unless there is mingling of blood. We owe it to the posterity of both races that this experiment be not tried, in either America or Japan. ... There is, perhaps unfortunately, no physical repugnance between the white and yellow races, and even if there were, the mulatto population of America is a tragic proof that the most powerful racial repulsion, aided by a fiercely guarded social line, is not sufficient to prevent amalgamations.

This is the Japanese end of the question, which is acute because Japan is powerful and awake. ... The whole situation challenges this generation in America to answer the question: Where shall be the frontier of the white man's world?

Chester H. Rowell, "Orientophobia: A Western Editor's Views on the White Frontier," _Collier's_ 42 (February 6, 1909).

In Their Own Words

Poems Written on the Walls of Angel Island Dormitories

Chinese immigrants wrote these unsigned poems on the walls of the Angel Island detention station, near San Francisco, California. The immigrants were kept there until they could prove they had relatives in America, and until it was shown that they had no diseases.

The west wind ruffles my thin gauze clothing.

On the hill sits a tall building with a room of wooden planks.

I wish I could travel on a cloud far away, reunite with my wife and son.

When the moonlight shines on me alone, the nights seem even longer.

At the head of the bed there is wine and my heart is constantly drunk.

There is no flower beneath my pillow and my dreams are not sweet.

To whom can I confide my innermost feelings?

I rely solely on close friends to relieve my loneliness.

The insects chirp outside the four walls.

The inmates often sigh.

Thinking of affairs back home,

Unconscious tears wet my lapel.

America has power, but not justice.

In prison, we were victimized as if we were guilty.

Given no opportunity to explain, it was really brutal.

I bow my head in reflection but there is nothing I can do.

For what reason must I sit in jail?

It is only because my country is weak and my family poor.

My parents wait at the door but there is no news.

My wife and child wrap themselves in quilt, sighing with loneliness.

Even if my petition is approved and I can enter the country,

When can I return to the Mountains of Tang with a full load?

From ancient times, those who venture out usually become worthless.

How many people ever return from battles?

In Dorothy Hoobler and Thomas Hoobler, *The Chinese American Family Album* (New York: Oxford University Press, 1994).

We Change — Traditions Remain

All people and cultures use art, food, storytelling, music, and drama to express their feelings, personality, and values. Think of the difference between Japanese or Korean music and African music. Think of the difference between flowing, detailed Chinese papercuts and the geometric shapes that appear in Navajo sandpainting or weaving. Think of the difference between the lyrical nature of much Korean writing and the more naturalistic writing of Europeans and Americans.

Traditions, whether music for the ear, food for the body, or stories for the soul, are called folkways. Folkways are important expressions of every culture and nation. Folkways keep heritage and history alive. They are bridges from one generation to the next. For immigrants, folkways are bridges to their homeland; links to the memories, people, and traditions of the past. Folkways carry on the traditions of a people from one generation to the next.

Japanese, Chinese, and Korean people often use and make lanterns. This is not unique, since Swedish people make lanterns of tin and Egyptians use lanterns of brass or pottery. However, the Asian lanterns are paper. They spread light and color at the same time. They are delicate and three dimensional. Lanterns appear at parties, festivals, and in family homes.

Japanese art is known for its control and attention to detail. Bonkei, or tray landscapes, and flower arranging are popular crafts. Haiku and senryu poetry is very structured, with exact numbers of syllables and lines in each poem. Where Americans sometimes think art has to be free, the Japanese see beauty in rules and forms. While some Japanese artists create "free" art, others are challenged to create beautiful, original works while following a set of rules.

In Japan, Korea, and China, traditional figures and forms appear in weaving, painting, theatre, stories, and crafts. In China, for example, cranes, pine trees, and lotus flowers all have symbolic meanings. In Korea, dogs, ducks, and other animals figure prominently. Colors have meaning as well. And writing in China, Korea, and Japan is both symbolic and artistic.

Around the world, art, food, and folkways are part of religious and cultural holidays and festivals. It is no different in East Asia. All three cultures studied here have traditional holiday celebrations. Dragon masks appear at every celebration of the new year.

Korean, Japanese, and Chinese immigrants in the United States have kept many of their traditions. Especially in Chinese communities, holidays are celebrated with public displays of fireworks, music, and costumes. Japanese families still prepare special foods to honor their ancestors. And many Japanese and Chinese crafts are taught to people of all ethnic backgrounds in communities across America.

Folkways in a Nation of Immigrants

The following projects will help you learn about the traditions and folkways of East Asian immigrants. Learning and enjoying the art, food, stories, music, drama, and crafts of other cultures is like opening a window into the history and heritage of other people. You will experience traditions still practiced in East Asia today. And you will learn to appreciate traditions practiced by your neighbors and fellow Americans.

❦ Your teacher has instructions for making a traditional Chinese New Year dragon head/costume. This can be made as a hand puppet or large enough to be worn on a person's head. Make a dragon head. Read about the Chinese New Year celebration and tell your class what you learn.

❦ Prepare the recipe for fried rice found in this unit. Or find and prepare another East Asian recipe. Bring your dish in for the class to sample. When you shop for ingredients, find containers of Asian sauces and spices. Note the ingredients and bring a list of unusual items you find to class.

❦ Your teacher has instructions for writing haiku and senryu, traditional forms of Japanese poetry. Follow the directions and write some haiku and senryu. Share your poems with the class. This project can be done in pairs or as a group exercise

❦ Find out about the history of origami. Learn to make at least five origami figures. What do the figures mean? Teach an origami figure to your class and tell them what you have learned.

❦ Learn about Bonkei. In this art, Japanese craftspeople make small, detailed diorama-like gardens. Using papier mâché and soil, sand, grass, and paint, make a Bonkei tray garden to show the class.

❦ Paper cutting is an ancient Chinese tradition. Learn how paper cutting is done. Read about the history of paper cutting in China. Tell your class what you have learned.

❦ Print making is especially common in Chinese art. Use your library to find traditional designs. Carve your design into a block of balsa wood, linoleum, or styrofoam. Make prints to show your class. Your art teacher may be able to help you with equipment for carving or print making. **NOTE: This project requires the use of knives and sharp tools. It should only be done with the help or supervision of a teacher, parent, or other adult.**

❦ Interview cooks at a Korean, Japanese, and Chinese restaurant. Ask them to describe the differences among the cooking styles in each country and culture. Get a recipe from each cook. Prepare one at home and bring in the dish for your class to sample.

❦ Learn and tell a Korean, Japanese, or Chinese folktale.

❦ See the project idea for shadow puppets listed in Writing and Research Topics.

❦ Use library or on-line resources to learn about Japanese, Korean, or Chinese writing. Learn how to write words or phrases. Bring examples in to show your class. Using a brush and ink or tempera paint, copy calligraphy examples. Can you find enough examples of words and phrases to "build"sentences? Find examples of Japanese, Korean, or Chinese writing. See if you can find symbols you recognize. Present what you discover to the class.

Folkways in a Nation of Immigrants

Dragon Head

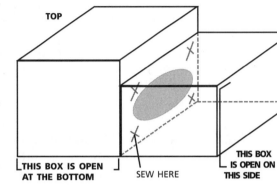

TOP

THIS BOX IS OPEN AT THE BOTTOM

SEW HERE

THIS BOX IS OPEN ON THIS SIDE

The Chinese and other Asians celebrate the New Year with parades featuring dragons and lions. A simple kind of homemade lion or dragon head can be made out of cardboard boxes, wire, tape, and paint.

MATERIALS NEEDED:

2 cardboard boxes –
one a little larger than the other

bailing wire

paper tape

paint and brushes

small saw or cutting knife

extra cardboard for horns, eyes, and tongue

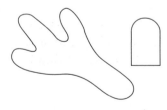

EYE
(cut 2" – 8" long)

HORN
cut 2" – 24" long)

Note: You can make a miniature version for use as a hand puppet.

1. Place the two boxes together. The larger box has the open side down. The smaller box opens to the front side. Attach the boxes with wire by poking holes in the boxes at the **X**s, and "sewing" them together with the wire.

2. Using the paper tape, tape around all the cracks where the two boxes connect. If you are using the kind of paper tape you have to wet, it is best to dip cut pieces in water, then smooth them to the cardboard using a sponge to absorb the extra water. If you wipe the paper tape with a wet sponge to moisten, you often wipe off the glue.

3. Add horns and eyes in the same way. Cut them from extra cardboard with the small saw or cutting knife. Sew them on with wire then cover them with paper tape.

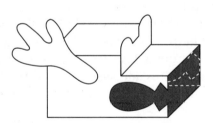

4. When everything is really dry — the next day — cut out the mouth with the saw or knife. Also cut out the hole inside the mouth so you can see out when you play the head. (Note gray oval in drawing #1.) Be sure to cut mouth on both sides.

5. Paint the dragon. Traditional colors are green with red, white, black, and yellow. Horns should be yellow. Around the mouth there should be a pattern like the one shown here. Paint the eyes last. Tradition says that when you "dot the dragon's eye," *he comes to life.*

6. Make a tail from a long piece of decorated cloth. Use about 1½ yards of cloth for each person who will carry the tail in the parade. Attach the tail to the back of the head with wire, or sew with string.

7. One person can now wear the dragon head and lead the parade. Other people can follow behind, carrying and waving the dragon's tail.

Folkways in a Nation of Immigrants

Fried Rice

This simple recipe from China is best prepared in a wok, a large metal pan with a rounded bottom. The rounded bottom enables heat to travel quickly and evenly along the sides of the wok. A large skillet can substitute for a wok. Stir-frying is a common Chinese cooking technique. All ingredients are prepared in advance. Ingredients are chopped into bite-sized pieces to ensure even and fast cooking. Then, oil is added to the wok over high heat. After the oil is hot, ingredients are quickly stirred together.

INGREDIENTS

3 tablespoons cooking oil

1 can chickpeas

1 egg beaten (to reduce cholesterol, remove the egg yolk)

2 tablespoons chopped green onions (scallions)

⅓ cup diced mushrooms

⅓ cup peas

⅓ cup carrots, boiled until soft

2½ cups cooked rice

dash of pepper

soy sauce, to taste

1. Heat the wok or skillet.

2. Add the oil and rotate the wok briefly to spread the oil around the bottom and sides of the wok.

3. When the oil is hot, pour in the beaten egg and stir-fry until it solidifies.

4. Add scallions, mushrooms, peas, and carrots. Stir-fry lightly.

5. Add cooked rice and pepper.

6. Stir-fry until rice is brown.

7. Remove from heat and add soy sauce.

Serves 4.

Optional:
For variety, add one of the following after stir-frying vegetables:
½ cup cooked chicken, pork, beef, or shrimp.

Folkways in a Nation of Immigrants

Haiku and Senryu: *Poetic Forms from Japan*

Two of the most popular poetic styles in Japan, and around the world, are haiku and senryu. They have the same form: both consist of 17 syllables. (Syllables are the groups of sounds that make up words. The word "word" has one syllable; the word "syl-la-ble" has three syllables.) All you have to do to write a haiku or a senryu is to write a poem of exactly 17 syllables. You don't have to do rhymes.

What's the difference between the two? Haiku are about nature and always let you know what season the poem is talking about. Senryu do not; they are generally more concerned with people's daily lives than with seasons. Look at the two poems below:

> **Brown leaf fell on this girl's head**
> **As we walked to school —**
> **Nobody told her.**

> **Light turns green**
> **But I don't move.**
> **Go ahead and honk:**
> **I do what I want.**

We see that the first poem mentions a brown leaf falling. Since leaves usually turn brown and fall in the autumn, we know that this poem is a haiku. The second poem could take place at any time of year, so it is a senryu.

In the poems below, mark the haiku with H and the senryu with S.

> **Do bugs have eyebrows?**
> **Am I the only person**
> **Who's ever asked this?**

> **He wears his sweatshirt**
> **On August's hottest day and**
> **Man! Is he sweating!**

> **She was smiling but**
> **I don't think she was happy:**
> **Sun in the winter.**

> **Where'd you get that bike?**
> **Hey, that looks like my old bike.**
> **Hey, you stole my bike!**

Now: write your own!

Exercise 1. Write one haiku on each of the following subjects. Then get a partner and compare poems. What's similar about your partner's poems? What's different about them?

> **icy street**   **fog**   **thunderstorm**   **spring rain**

Exercise 2. Same as above, but it's senryu time! Here are your topics:

> **broccoli**   **toothache**   **fish**   **homework**

Exercise 3. Complete the following poem as a haiku. Compare your ending with your partner's ending:

> **Yellow dog in snow....**

Research & Writing Topics

The following list includes suggestions for individual or group research and writing projects for this unit on immigrants from East Asia

❧ Choose a fiction book about Japanese, Chinese, or Korean life in America. Write a book report telling the class about the story and its meaning to you.

❧ Trace a large map of the East Asian region. Using magazines, photocopied pictures from library and reference books, and on-line graphics, find pictures of as many cultural/ethnic groups in China, Japan, and Korea as possible. Look especially for illustrations of national costumes, traditions, or cultural lifestyles. Attach pictures to show where different groups live. Write captions under your photos giving information about the ethnic group, its people, traditions, and unique ways.

❧ Find out about the important part played by Chinese immigrants in the building of America's railroads. Tell why Chinese immigrants came to America, how they lived, and what their experiences were on the railroad crews.

❧ What was the Boxer Rebellion? How did it affect China? How did it affect Chinese immigration to America?

❧ Find out about Chinese immigrants' involvement in the gold rush. Tell about the quest for gold in California and the experiences of Chinese immigrants.

❧ Chinese folktales are filled with common symbols and images. Read some traditional folktales and retell them in your own words. Learn and tell about the common symbols and their meanings. Illustrate one folktale and tell it aloud to the class.

❧ How did the experience of Chinese immigrants compare to the experience of Africans brought to America as slaves? Consider similarities and differences. Consider how the physical features of these two groups of people influenced their experiences. Learn how both groups came to America. How were those experiences similar and different?

❧ Find out about the internment of Japanese Americans during World War Two. What happened? Why did the U.S. government act in this manner? How did this affect Japanese Americans? If you had lived then, would you have agreed or disagreed with the government's actions? Why? What do you think was done right? What mistakes do you think were made?

❧ Learn about Japanese religion and family life. Learn about cultural rules in Japan, such as respect for elders, treatment of women, and veneration of ancestors. How did those traditions affect the way Japanese immigrants lived in America? How did they influence the feelings Japanese immigrants had about America? Can you think of ways in which American thoughts and attitudes would be different, even offensive, to Japanese immigrants?

Research & Writing Topics

East Asia

❦ Learn about Chinese "paper sons," men who posed as the sons of Chinese immigrants in order to gain entry into the U.S. Who were "paper sons"? When did they come over? How did the system work? How did U.S. immigration officials try to identify them? What was their experience? Write a report on what you learn.

❦ Before the 1960s, Korean immigrants were almost unknown in this country. Today, some experts say there are nearly a million people of Korean ancestry living here. Why did Koreans move here? Why did they settle most often in large cities? What occupations do they hold? Have these occupations caused them problems? How?

❦ Early Chinese, Japanese, and Korean immigrant men relied on "picture brides" to start a family in the United States. The "picture bride" system was designed to evade U.S. immigration laws, which forbade nearly all Asian immigration. How did the system work? Who were the "picture brides"? What was their fate in America?

❦ This topic combines the research/writing portion of this unit with a folkways project. Find a Japanese, Chinese, or Korean folktale that could be told to younger children. Learn about shadow puppets using the library or other resources. Write a short report about shadow puppet design, history, and use in Japan or China. Then design and make shadow puppets for this folktale and perform the tale for your class. Take your show on the road, performing the folktale for classes of younger children and giving those classes information about shadow puppetry.

Southeast Asia

NOTE TO TEACHERS:
The materials on the
student pages that
follow are intended to
provide your students
with background,
project ideas, and
topics for research.
You may choose to
share some or all of
these pages directly
with your students.
Or you may choose to
adapt and format
them to fit your own
schedule, curriculum,
and philosophy.
This unit also includes
craft instructions that
you can photocopy
and distribute to
your students.

This unit on Southeast Asian immigrants focuses on the three mainland nations of Cambodia, Vietnam, and Laos, and on the island nation of the Philippines.

These nations are not alone on the culturally diverse peninsula south of China and east of India. But most of the Southeast Asian immigrants to the U.S. have come from these countries.

Teachers may wish to inform students that immigrants have come from other Southeast Asian and Asian nations as well. Many people have fled religious and political persecution in Indonesia. The reunification of Hong Kong with mainland China has been the catalyst for yet another wave of Asian immigrants seeking refuge in the U.S.

Studying this region may raise sensitive issues and deep feelings related to the conflict in Vietnam. Teachers may consider viewing films such as *The Killing Fields* because of their historical value. *The Killing Fields* and similar films provide important information and insights. However, use of these films must be carefully considered. They are extremely violent and may be unacceptable to many students and parents. Their content is inappropriate for immature and young students.

The following ideas would enhance and further develop this unit:

❧ Invite a Laotian, Cambodian, or Vietnamese member of your community to speak to the class. Ask them to tell about their experiences in leaving their country and coming here.

❧ Invite a Filipino student or member or your community to speak to your class about life in the Philippines. Ask them to tell the story of their own emigration, including how, when, and why they came to the U.S. Ask if this individual could demonstrate Tinikling dance, share words in the Tagalog language, or bring photos of his or her family and life in the Philippines.

❧ If Cambodians live in your area, invite some women to demonstrate their traditional dancing.

❧ If Hmong — (MUNG) — live in your area, ask a Hmong woman to bring in samples of *pa'ndau* — (pan dow) — and talk about this craft and how she learned it.

❧ Ask students whose own ethnic background is Southeast Asian to interview their parents and grandparents about when, where, why, and how their families immigrated to the U.S. Or invite their relatives to come and share their experiences with the class.

☙ Bring in films or audio tapes to share music, dance, and drama from this region.

☙ Set aside a single time for students to share food, crafts, and projects from the We Change — Traditions Remain and Folkways in a Nation of Immigrants portions of this unit.

Why They Came to America

The following is a brief history of the people who came to the United States from Southeast Asia — the Philippines, Vietnam, Laos, and Cambodia.

THE PHILIPPINES The Philippines is a group of nearly 7,000 islands off the southeast coast of Asia. In 1521, the Spanish explorer Ferdinand Magellan was the first European to arrive at the island chain. After 50 years of fighting, the Spanish conquered the islands and named them for King Philip. From 1570 to 1898, the Spanish ruled the islands as a colony. In 1898, the United States took the Philippines from Spain after the Spanish-American War. For five years after that, U.S. troops fought against Filipinos who wanted their country to be independent. The U.S. Army gained control of the Philippines and ruled it as a colony. After nearly 40 years of relative peace, World War Two began. During the war, Americans and Filipinos fought together against the Japanese, who occupied the islands.

Since 1907, Filipinos have left their country for the United States in order to escape poverty. At first, many settled in Hawaii, but soon, they also traveled to the mainland U.S. Between 1907 and 1930, about 50,000 Filipinos, most of them agricultural workers, came to America. Since World War Two, thousands of Filipinos have immigrated to America. Many of them are professionals, especially doctors, nurses, and technicians. Filipinos have come here to escape poverty and the frequently unstable political situation in their home country, to become educated, and to find work.

The largest Filipino population in the United States is in Los Angeles. Other areas of the West Coast also have large Filipino populations. However, people of Filipino heritage are scattered throughout the U.S., mostly in urban areas.

VIETNAM, LAOS, AND CAMBODIA Before 1975, there were few immigrants from these countries in the United States. Today, there are more than 700,000. Nearly all these immigrants were refugees — that is, they fled their country because they were in danger of losing their lives due to terrible wars and the unstable governments in their countries.

In 1975, North Vietnam won a long and bitter war against South Vietnam and its ally, the United States. The North Vietnamese were led by communists who took over all of Vietnam. Because of this, thousands of Vietnamese left their country any way they could, bound for camps in Thailand, Indonesia, and the Philippines. Soon, these refugees were taken in by countries all over the world, but mostly by the United States.

In 1976, a group called the Khmer Rouge took over Cambodia. They treated the people of Cambodia very cruelly. The violent upheavals in Vietnam and Cambodia led to unrest in Laos as well. Soon, a second wave of refugees from Cambodia and Laos escaped their countries and took the same route that Vietnamese refugees had taken to the U.S. and other countries.

Why They Came to America

All these refugees faced incredible hardships all along the way. They risked death escaping from their home countries, traveling in rickety boats that often capsized or were attacked by pirates. Once they reached the refugee camps, they had to wait months or years before they found a place to resettle. Their settlement in the U.S. was also difficult. Culture clashes between the land they left and the one they came to created new challenges. Today, Southeast Asians are scattered in small settlements throughout the United States. Some are unable to read or speak English, while others are college students and successful businesspeople. Many of them are farmers, fishermen, and craftspeople.

In Their Own Words

NOTE TO TEACHERS:

In this section, immigrants to the U.S. tell about their experiences coming to and living in America.

On these pages, we have reprinted the stories of two girls, one from Cambodia and one from Vietnam. After reading their stories, you might discuss with your class the difference between an immigrant and a refugee. A discussion about the hardships these girls and their families faced — both in their home countries and in the United States — might also be helpful. You might also want to talk about the following questions:

How do you think you would have handled the situations these girls found themselves in? What do you think it was like for them to come to a new country? What are some similarities and differences in their stories?

In Their Own Words

The Story of My Life

The following is by a young girl named Thuoy Chom who escaped from Cambodia with her family and settled in the United States in the late 1970s. This piece was written when she was twelve years old.

My name is Thuoy Chom. My father's name is Sovainn Chom. My mother's name is Novn. I have four sisters. Their names are Theap, Thoeung, Sophon, and Maney.

Theap is the oldest. I am the next. My older sister, myself, and Thoeung were born in Cambodia. Sophon was born in Thailand, and Maney was born in the United States.

When I was three, war broke out in Cambodia. School closed. Everything closed. My dad was a soldier. He didn't want to shoot and kill other Cambodians. A meeting was held. My father was asked to attend. At this meeting, he was told that within three days he and his family would be killed.

Quickly our dad planned our escape. He chopped down trees and used the logs to build a wagon. Under our house were some old wheels. Soon the wagon was finished and at night our family got in the wagon and set off for Thailand.

One mile from the house, the wagon broke down. We left the wagon which was impossible to repair, and the two bulls who were pulling it, and continued on foot. We had no shoes so walking was difficult. My dad carried Theap and me. My mother carried Thoeung. The ground was rough. Both my parents got thorns in their feet.

Soon the Khmer Rouge [the Cambodian government] were following us. They were the enemy from which we were escaping. My dad had his gun and three small bombs. Twice he had to throw bombs in the path behind us. Soon we were able to continue for a time undisturbed.

We were traveling through a thick, hilly jungle. Then we met a group composed of two other families. They were also escaping to Thailand. Our families whispered about the plans of escape. Companions on the escape trip our parents thought would be helpful. Because my sisters and I were so young, the other families did not want us to travel with them. They even suggested to my parents that we be left in the jungle alone. My parents would not do this, so we continued our escape separately.

The two other families set off down the next hill. Both my parents were so tired. We had to be carried, so they were extra tired. We stopped to rest. At the foot of the hill, and within our sight, the two other families were captured and killed by the Khmer Rouge soldiers. We waited quietly for the enemy to leave. My sisters and I did not make a sound. Thoeung wanted to cry, but my mother was able to keep her quiet by nursing her.

In Their Own Words

When morning came we went down the hill. The jungle was one hill after another. As we walked along we ate berries, and fish my dad caught in the stream. We also found small red apples. My dad knew which wild food was poison.

Eventually our family got to Thailand. In Thailand we searched for our uncle, and eventually found him. He had a big house where we could live. He found my dad a job in a windmill. My aunt took care of Theoung who was only three months old. My mother worked in the fields harvesting rice.

My older sister and I went to school. Here we liked school. Our teacher was called sister, and she called her students little sisters and little brothers. We wore uniforms. The girls were dressed in blue and white, and the boys in green and white. We were happy in Thailand.

Our grandparents were still in Cambodia, and we missed them. My father decided to return to get them. My uncle went, too.

My dad and uncle put on their old uniforms. Perhaps no one had missed them. When they got close to our grandparents' home, they were captured and sent to jail. They were given very little food to eat. After two or three months my uncle was able to leave the jail and get outside where he started to pick some leaves to eat. He was shot and killed by the guard.

My dad was starving. He also tried to get into the yard surrounding the jail to look for food. He started to dig up what he thought was a potato. It was a bomb and it exploded. His leg was injured.

My mother heard of my father's injuries. She left Thailand to return to Cambodia. She brought food and money. She paid the guards and they released my dad. He returned to Thailand with our mother. When his leg healed, he set off for Cambodia again, to try to rescue our grandparents. Again he was captured, and my mother again came to pay the guards.

Our family stayed in Thailand for two years. Then we came to the United States. First we made our home in Chicago, and then in Evanston [Illinois]. The people here are kind to us and the neighborhood is pleasant. I like school. I'm happy. Now I'm remembering my past life and writing about it.

In Their Own Words

**Written by
Rosie Truong,
a Vietnamese
immigrant who
moved to California
when she was
three years old.**

Narrative of a Vietnamese Immigrant

When I was little, I asked my mother, "What was Vietnam like?" She replied with a question: "What do you remember?"

I only remember getting on a plane and being scared. I remember holding my mother's hand so tightly and wondering where my dad was.

April 1975: My mother had my three-month-old sister on one arm and a duffel bag strapped onto her other arm. I was holding on to my mother's hand as we were boarding a military plane to leave Vietnam. An American man offered to hold my sister to help my mother. I started to scream and cry because I didn't want my sister to be taken away. Being only three years old and not understanding what was going on, I continued to scream when the man offered to hold her duffel bag instead. I just wanted him to leave us alone. My mother told me that the flight was very long, but we going to a much better place.

We finally landed in Guam. This is where we stayed for three days with other refugees. On the fourth day we continued our journey. We came to America — Camp Pendleton, California — our first stop to our new lives.

Two weeks went by before my father came to the camp to find us. My father worked for the Vietnamese government at the time, so he was not allowed to leave the country with us. I was too young to understand back then, but my father married an American woman so that he would legally be able to leave Vietnam. She was a very nice woman, a family friend, who agreed to help us. Now our family was back together and we could start our new lives.

My dad moved our family out of the refugee camp and straight down south to Escondido, California. My dad's first job in America was as a deliveryman. He delivered eggs all day long with a friend he made at the camp. My dad said that he would always bring home dozens of eggs for us. Pretty soon, we were all quite sick of eggs!

My mom stayed home to take care of us kids. My sister Mai Huong was too small for my mom to leave every day so she could work. So, we stayed home for about a year until my dad saved up enough money so we could move to Los Angeles. L.A. seemed like the place where things happened for my parents and life was simple and carefree for me. We moved into a very small studio apartment in the heart of downtown L.A. For the next few years, my parents went to school, worked, and raised their young family.

Thinking back, I know my parents worked very hard to make their dreams come true. We were a young family who had lots of hurdles in

In Their Own Words

front of us. My dad had decent English skills, but my mom had to take E.S.L. [English as a Second Language] classes. My mom worked as a cashier in an outlet store, a few blocks away from home. I think my mom learned how to speak Spanish before she learned English.

As for me, life was pretty easy. When I was four, I started a preschool program called Head Start. School was fun. My babysitter was this old Mexican lady whom I called Concha. My sister and I were afraid of her. She was old and we couldn't understand her. She spoke Spanish and we spoke Vietnamese. She never allowed us to do anything except play in the living room until my mom came to pick us up. Concha used to walk me to school and back every day.

One day, she mentioned to my mom that I got "*mejillas rojas*" ("rosy cheeks") from walking in the sun after school. Concha also told my mom that she calls me "Mejillas Rojas" because she couldn't call me by my Vietnamese name. Shortly after my first parent-teacher conference, my mom told me my American name was Rosie. My mom was told that my teacher also had trouble pronouncing my Vietnamese name, Mai Khanh. My teacher suggested giving me a nickname like Pinky. She thought that because I was half the size of all the other preschoolers, Pinky was a cute and appropriate nickname for me. I'm glad my mom decided on Rosie.

My parents knew that they wanted their daughters to be the best, which meant sacrificing their time being newlyweds, working during the day and going to school at night, and picking out the right name for Rosie.

We Change — Traditions Remain

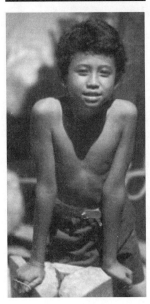

Traditions, whether music for the ear, food for the body, or stories for the soul, are called folkways. Folkways are important expressions of every culture and nation. Folkways keep heritage and history alive. They are bridges from one generation to the next. For immigrants, folkways are bridges to their homeland; links to the memories, people, and traditions of the past. Folkways carry on the traditions of a people from one generation to the next.

Many tribes and cultural groups in Southeast Asia have been influenced by China. Buddhism's Chinese roots have an influence in these countries. Some tribes, such as the Hmong, came from China originally. Cambodia's Khmer people trace their ancestors to China, Tibet, and Indonesia. Common Chinese themes can be found in Vietnamese art, Laotian needlework, and Cambodian silks.

Language has influenced art and folkways in Southeast Asia. The Hmong people in Laos, Cambodia, and Vietnam create a unique kind of needlework called *pa'ndau*, or flower cloths. For many centuries, the Hmong people had no written language. To tell their recent history, they have created embroidered "story cloths." In the last 40 years, the Hmong have used story cloths to tell folktales, and to relate the story of the terrible mass killings of their people by the Vietnamese communists. In a culture without written language, people tell their stories with a needle and thread.

The Vietnamese language also shows how language and art can form folk traditions. In Vietnamese, grammar is simple. For example, verbs don't change for past and present tense. Speakers simply add a word like "already" to show that an event occurred in the past. However, the language is rich with adjectives. Different words exist to show tiny differences in meaning.

Vietnamese people write, learn, recite, and admire poetry. Children and adults memorize long classical poems. When a couple is courting, it is expected that a Vietnamese young man will speak poetically. He might ask the girl if she will be the only flower in his garden. She might reply that her garden needs only a strong tree to be complete. During the Vietnam conflict, Buddhist monks used poetry to try to influence people against war.

Vietnam, Laos, and Cambodia were under the rule of other countries for centuries. The presence of Chinese, Japanese, French, and Indian occupants influenced traditions and culture. Silk embroidery patterns came from China. Laotian Hmong *pa'ndau* began there as well. French architecture and literature are common in Vietnam.

Many Southeast Asian people carve woodblocks for printing. Some common themes and images run through many of these carvings. In Vietnam, for example, a rice paddy, water buffalo, and a child playing the flute are all common scenes. Some experts think these images are comforting to a people with such a history of war and violence.

We Change — Traditions Remain

Cambodians are known for their rhythmic, flowing national dance, called *lamthon*. Even the youngest girls learn the traditional movements and symbolic hand motions. This type of dance is very ancient; the movements have not changed since the 15th century.

Laotian, Vietnamese, and Cambodian refugees have settled in many regions of the United States. In areas where many families have gathered, cultural clubs and organizations have begun to keep traditions and memories alive for young people. Like most immigrants, Southeast Asians settling in America have struggled to balance the old with the new. Their children are becoming more and more American. And elders are growing concerned as young people lose interest in their traditions and heritage. Even now, across the United States, Southeast Asian communities are learning what it means to be Laotian, Vietnamese, or Khmer and Americans, too.

Off the coast of Vietnam, the thousands of islands that make up the Republic of the Philippines are home to more than 80 separate ethnic groups. Each brings unique crafts, music, folklore, and traditions to contribute to the culture of the Philippines.

Wood carving and weaving are crafts practiced in most Philippine tribes and ethnic groups. Filipino wood carving is known throughout the world.

Over the years, the Philippines have also been ruled by many governments from other lands. The islands were a colony of Japan, Spain, and the U.S. for more than 400 years. Each country left behind languages, religious and other traditions, foods, music, and arts that affected the way Filipino culture grew and developed. Tagalog, a version of a native mountain dialect, and English are both national languages. Many names have Spanish origins, and Filipino traditional dance is similar to dances done in Cambodia.

Folkways in a Nation of Immigrants

The following projects will help you learn about the traditions and folkways of Southeast Asian immigrants. Learning and enjoying the art, food, stories, music, drama, and crafts of other cultures is like opening a window into the history and heritage of other people. You will experience traditions still practiced in Southeast Asia today. And you will learn to appreciate traditions practiced by your neighbors and fellow Americans.

❦ Prepare the recipe for Vietnamese *goi cuon,* or spring rolls, found in this unit. Or choose another recipe from Cambodia, Laos, Vietnam, or the Philippines. Share your dish with the class. What interesting spices did you discover?

❦ Learn about *pa'ndau,* or flower cloths, a traditional type of needlework done by women from the Hmong tribes. *Pa'ndau* done by Laotian Hmong can be found in many parts of the U.S. today. Find out why *pa'ndau* is important to Hmong culture. If possible, interview a Hmong person about the meaning of *pa'ndau.* Choose one of the *pa'ndau* patterns available from your teacher. You can use colored paper or cloth, scissors, and glue to create an example of *pa'ndau* of your own. Finally, write a report and share what you learn with the class.

❦ Learn about Hmong story cloths, which are different from *pa'ndau.* Find a folktale and create a Hmong-style story cloth to tell the story in pictures. You may glue cut paper or cloth, or you may draw your story cloth on a large sheet of paper. Tell the story to the class using your story cloth.

❦ Find a traditional Vietnamese poem translated into English. Memorize it and recite it to the class. Read about Vietnamese poetry and tell the class what you learn.

❦ Lacquerware is made all over Southeast Asia. Find pictures of lacquerware. Using papier-mâché, make a bowl. Paint it using the colors and images you find in traditional lacquerware.

❦ Using papier-mâché or clay, make a topographical map of the countries in this unit. Explain how you think the geography of Southeast Asia has affected its history and the way people live.

❦ Traditional homes in Cambodian villages are unique. Find out how they are made and why. Make a model of a traditional Cambodian home.

❦ Visit area import shops or museum stores. Take a camera along. Find examples and take pictures of wood carving, weaving, cloth, and jade sculpture from the Philippines. Take photos of clothing, embroidery, wood carving, or prints from any of the other countries in this unit. Show your photos to the class.

❦ Learn about Filipino wood carving, an ancient craft valued around the world. What are traditional carving patterns? What do these patterns and symbols mean? What types of wood are used? How important is wood carving to the Philippine economy? Find photos or examples of Filipino carvers' work to show the class.

❦ Find a folktale from any of the four countries studied in this unit. Learn the story to tell aloud to the class.

Folkways in a Nation of Immigrants

Goi Cuon (Fresh Spring Rolls)

This recipe for an appetizer or snack comes from Vietnam. "Goi cuon" literally means "salad wrap."

1. Immerse a sheet of rice paper in cold water. Lie flat.

2. Place two shrimp halves in the center of the rice paper.

3. Put a pinch of rice vermicelli over shrimp.

4. Put a pinch of herbs (mint and cilantro) over vermicelli.

5. Put a pinch of lettuce over herbs.

6. Put a pinch of sprouts over lettuce.

7. Carefully roll rice paper into a roll. Repeat for each sheet of rice paper.

Serve with dipping sauce (below).

Makes 3 spring rolls.

INGREDIENTS

3 sheets rice paper

6 cooked halved shrimp

⅛ cup chopped mint and ⅛ cup cilantro

¼ cup beansprouts

2 ounces rice vermicelli

3 red leaf lettuce leaves, sliced julienne-style

Dipping Sauce

Mix ingredients well. Chili paste will make dipping sauce hot and spicy.

INGREDIENTS for Dipping Sauce

4 tablespoons hoisin sauce (black bean paste)

1 tablespoon water

1 tablespoon coconut milk

½ teaspoon chili paste (optional)

Folkways in a Nation of Immigrants

Pa'ndau Designs

Below are some examples of traditional Hmong *pa'ndau*, or flower cloth patterns. Use colored paper or cloth, scissors, and glue to create a *pa'ndau* of your own. To the left you can see an example of a finished *pa'ndau*.

Star

Snail

Heart

Elephant foot

Steps

Crab claw

Single-center diamond

Triangle

Cucumber seed

Spider web/star

Snail center diamonds

Mountains

Cucumber seeds

Dragon tail/ rooster comb

Maze

3 Motif

Elaborate steps

Research & Writing Topics

The following list includes suggestions for individual or group research and writing projects for this unit on immigrants from Southeast Asia

❦ The Hmong people live in Laos, Cambodia, Vietnam, and Thailand. The Laotian Hmong have come to America as refugees. Learn about their history. Find out why they left Laos, their relationship with the American military, where they fled for safety, and how they came to the United States. Trace the route taken by Laotian Hmong from their homeland to Thailand on a map. Write a report about what you learn. Summarize the information and, using your map, present it to the class.

❦ Create a timeline showing the history of the Vietnam conflict. Learn about the Ho Chi Minh Trail, Viet Cong, guerrilla warfare, American advisors, Agent Orange, tunnel rats, the Tet offensive, Rolling Thunder, napalm, and the fall of Saigon. Give a report to your class on what you learn.

❦ Trace a large map of Southeast Asia. Using magazines, photocopied pictures from libraries and reference books, and on-line graphics, find illustrations of as many cultural/ethnic groups in this region as possible. Look especially for pictures of national costumes, traditions, or cultural lifestyles. Attach pictures to show where people live. Write captions under your photos giving information about each ethnic group, its people, traditions, and unique ways.

❦ Interview someone who served in the Vietnam conflict. Learn why the U.S. government considered the war worth fighting. What were the issues involved? What happened? Find out about the experience, thoughts, and feelings of the person you interview. Write a report and share what you've learned with the class.

❦ Interview someone who protested against the conflict in Vietnam. Find out why this person opposed the war. Learn about the person's experience and his or her thoughts and reflections now. Learn about the war moratorium, the draft lottery, and the eventual withdrawal of U.S. soldiers. Write a report and share your information with the class.

❦ Find out about the history of the Vietnam Memorial in Washington, D.C. When was it built? Why did the artist who created it design the monument the way she did? Why did veterans think a memorial was needed? Some people called it "the homecoming I never had." Find out why they felt this way. Write a report about the information you learn. Present it orally to the class, using photos when possible.

❦ Learn about the history of prisoners of war and people missing in action (POW-MIAs) from the Vietnam conflict. Why were people not found? Why do some people think Americans may still be held prisoner in Southeast Asia? What has the government done about the POW-MIA issue? Write a report and share with the class what you discover.

Research & Writing Topics

Southeast Asia

- Learn about the civil war in Cambodia. Write a report on the history of this war. Present it orally to the class. Use maps, photos, reference books, and news articles whenever possible. Find out about the following people, places, and things, and why they were important to Cambodia:
  Khmer Rouge, Kampuchea, Phnom Penh, Pol Pot, The Killing Fields, Mekong River, Thailand

- Who were the Southeast Asian boat people? Find out about the history of these refugees. Learn how they left their homeland, what experiences they had along the way, and how many of them came to the United States. Write a report telling what you learn. Present it orally to the class.

- Learn about the sponsorship, immigration, and settlement of Vietnamese, Cambodian, and Laotian refugees in the U.S. during the 1970s and 1980s. Organizations like World Relief; the Salvation Army; the United Nations; or state, church, denominational, or community refugee assistance programs may be good sources of information. Write a report telling how people came from refugee camps to the U.S.

- What is the difference between refugees, like the people from Cambodia, Laos, or Vietnam, and other immigrants, like Filipinos who settled in America? Learn why and when Southeast Asian refugee groups came to America. Do you think the reasons people came to the United States influenced the way they adjusted to life in a new country? Why or why not? Find out about the Immigration and Naturalization Service process for people seeking asylum in the United States. Write a report telling what you learn. Present it orally to the class.

- The U.S. and the Philippines have had an unusual relationship since 1898. Find out more about this relationship and how it affected the immigration of Filipinos to the U.S. What is the state of the relationship today? How has it affected immigration?

- Ferdinand Marcos was once president of the Philippines. Learn about the Philippine government under his leadership. What was life like for the poor? For the wealthy? How many people came to the U.S. while he was president? Why do you think Filipinos might have left their country during this time? Write a report about what you learn.

- Learn about Benigno and Corazon Aquino. How did they affect life in the Philippines? How many people came to the U.S. when Ms. Aquino was president? Why do you think they left? Write or tell about what you learn.

- Find out about Dr. José Rizal, a famous Filipino author, doctor, poet, and historical figure. Find some examples of his writings, especially his poetry or letters, to read aloud in class. Find out what he did and how his life affected the history of the Philippines. Write or tell what you learn.

Research & Writing Topics

Southeast Asia

🐛 Learn about refugee camps in Thailand. The United Nations sponsored many camps. Church and international aid groups sponsored others. Where were they located? Why were they established? What did the Thai people think of the refugees and camps? Write a report telling what you discover. Share it with the class. Maps, photos, interviews, and news articles would be good additions to this project.

🐛 Choose a fiction book about life in Cambodia, Vietnam, Laos, or the Philippines, or about the lives of immigrants to America from Southeast Asia. Write a report about the story and its meaning to you. Present the report orally to the class.

🐛 Sticky rice? Basmati rice? Jasmine rice? Rice isn't just rice! Learn how rice is grown, harvested, and made ready for use. Consider why rice is so important in Southeast Asia. If oriental markets or restaurants are present in your community, visit one. Interview a cook or market owner to learn about the different kinds of rice. Learn how people from each country prepare and eat rice. Write a report and share what you learn with the class.

South Asia & the Middle East

NOTE TO TEACHERS:
The materials on the student pages that follow are intended to provide your students with background, project ideas, and topics for research. You may choose to share some or all of these pages directly with your students. Or you may choose to adapt and format them to fit your own schedule, curriculum, and philosophy.

This unit on South Asian and Middle Eastern immigration will focus on the nations of Armenia, Syria, Lebanon, India, and Pakistan.

Study of this region's immigrants will show an interesting variety of motivations for immigration to the United States. In Lebanon alone, for example, many immigrants sought economic opportunity. Others fled civil war. Still others, Christian and Muslim alike, were uncomfortable with the influence of Islamic fundamentalism on the government and sought religious freedom.

International political milestones, such as the ongoing Arab-Israeli conflicts, Iraqi aggression against Kuwait, and various Middle East peace agreements have influenced immigration. There is very little immigration from Israel to the United States, so in this unit, Israel is only mentioned as it relates to other countries in the Middle East. We have incorporated some topics on Judaism here because the Middle East is important to three of the world's major religions. Jewish immigration to the U.S. is explored extensively in the unit on Eastern Europe.

Understanding the influence of Islamic fundamentalism will challenge students. Piety and deeply-held religious convictions have become mixed with a revolutionary subculture within the greater Islamic community in the Middle East. Students will be encouraged to understand and separate the two ideas.

The place of women in Islamic society seems restricted to Western eyes. Students will also need to consider why some women have emigrated because of the doctrine of *chador* and separation of the sexes, while others remain.

In the South Asia, as in Africa and other developing nations, the issue of "brain drain" is a sensitive and difficult one. As highly educated citizens, often those with great potential for leadership and public service, immigrate to the United States in search of economic and vocational opportunities, countries experience "brain drain." Teachers may wish to open discussion of the implications of this pattern. Professors or students of South Asian descent from local universities may be available to discuss the issue with the class. The problem of "brain drain" also affects the Middle East.

In recent years, films and books have appeared dealing with the subject of Muslim-gentile marriages in America. Such productions tell the story of Western women married to Middle Eastern Muslims. In some situations, families have traveled to the Middle East and neither the women nor the children were permitted to return to the U.S. In others, fathers have taken their children to their Arab homelands and denied visitation to divorced wives.

Finally, since the people of the Middle East and South Asia cannot be understood apart from their religious perspectives, this unit includes some study of religious history, practices, doctrines, and influence upon government and personal lifestyles.

The following ideas would enhance and further develop this unit:

🐦 Invite a student from India, Pakistan, or the Middle East to visit your class.

🐦 Bring in a copy of the Koran in English and Arabic. Examine Arabic calligraphy. Read selections from the Koran aloud.

🐦 Collect and make available for extra reading appropriate magazines, including *National Geographic* back issues, that contain articles about South Asia or the Middle East.

🐦 Obtain tapes or CDs of Indian or Middle Eastern music. *Voices of Forgotten Worlds: Traditional Music of Indigenous People*, produced by Ellipsis Arts in 1993, contains, among other selections, interesting music from Bedouin culture.

🐦 View a film about the Middle East, the settlement of Israel, or a recent military conflict in the region.

🐦 Invite an Arab and a Jewish member of your community to speak about the conflict between their peoples in the Middle East. Care should be taken in selection of these individuals, since the subject matter is sensitive.

🐦 Show the film *Something Beautiful for God,* about Nobel Peace Prize recipient Mother Teresa's work among the poor and dying of Calcutta, India. Discuss the effect of such poverty on immigration.

🐦 Read selections from Rudyard Kipling's *The Jungle Book* aloud.

🐦 Invite a cantor from a synagogue or a reader from a Muslim mosque to visit the class.

🐦 Invite a Hindu to tell about Hindu beliefs, dietary laws, and traditions.

🐦 Invite someone with a background in history to discuss the Crusades, which were undertaken during the Medieval period to regain the Holy Land for Christianity.

🐦 Set aside a single time for students to share food, crafts, and projects from the We Change — Traditions Remain and Folkways in a Nation of Immigrants portions of this unit.

🐦 Ask if any students of South Asian or Middle Eastern background have relatives who immigrated to the U.S. Invite them to tell the class about their experience as immigrants.

Why They Came to America

The following is a brief history of the immigrant groups that came here from South Asia and the Middle East — India, Pakistan, Armenia, Syria, and Lebanon.

INDIA AND PAKISTAN At the turn of the century, a severe four-year drought hit the Punjab region of India. About 7,000 residents of Punjab — mostly Sikhs — traveled to America. They settled on the West Coast in California and Washington, where they took farming and logging jobs. The immigrants met a lot of hostility, and laws directed at all immigrants kept their numbers down for decades. In the meantime, two independent countries were carved from India's mainland — Pakistan and Bangladesh. Until the 1960s, immigration quotas severely limited the number of immigrants that could come to the U.S. from most countries. That changed with the Immigration Act of 1965, which eased quotas. As a result, more Asian Indians and Pakistanis made their way to the United States. Today, there are slightly fewer than a million people of Asian Indian and Pakistani descent living in the U.S. Many of them came for an education and stayed on to fill the need for highly-trained professionals in this country. Some of these professionals go back to their native lands, but the majority stay here and become citizens.

ARMENIA Between 1900 and 1914, nearly two million people of Armenian descent were massacred in their homelands in northern Turkey, and more than 50,000 Armenians came to America to escape persecution. The massacre started after some Armenians attempted to separate from Turkey and make an independent homeland. It continued as a new Turkish government tried to "purify" its country of non-Turkish elements. This event is called "The Great Massacre," and it is the first example of genocide in the 20th century. Genocide is the organized killing of an entire ethnic, religious, or racial population. The Great Massacre is still a source of bitterness between the Armenians and the Turks. Today, there are an estimated 500,000 people of Armenian descent living in the U.S.

SYRIA AND LEBANON There are more than two million Arab Americans in the United States. The numbers are not exact, however, because the thousands of Syrians and Lebanese who moved here in the 19th and early 20th century came here with Turkish passports. Until 1918, both Syria and Lebanon were part of the Turkish empire, and until 1941, Lebanon was part of Syria. The dominant religion in the Arab countries was, and remains, Islam, but the first Syrian/Lebanese immigrants to this country were Christians. They were members of the Melkite and Maronite Rites of the Roman Catholic Church, or members of the Syrian Orthodox Church. Immigrants came here to escape Turkish rule, and to practice their religion freely. Many of the first immigrants from Lebanon and Syria became peddlers. Door-to-door selling helped improve their knowledge of English. By 1919, there were an estimated 400,000 Syrian/Lebanese in this country, many of them settled in New York City.

Arab immigration has increased greatly since 1965. Now the dominant religion among Arab Americans is Islam. Large Arab populations can be found in many large urban centers.

In Their Own Words

NOTE TO TEACHERS:

The following documents relate the stories of recent immigrants from India. After reading their stories, you might want to discuss the following with your class.

The people in these narratives followed a pattern set by many immigrants. First, one or more members of a family come to this country, and when they are established here, they send for more members of their family. What challenges does an immigrant face if he or she is the first member of a family to reach the U.S.?

The first story talks about a young man coming to this country. Although he had help, he was expected to "sink or swim" while getting his education. Do you think this is a typical experience of immigrants? Do you think the man's professor was correct in treating him like any other student, or do you think some consideration should have been given a stranger in a foreign land?

The excerpt also describes how the author's mother was intimidated by supermarkets here — is hers a unique problem, or do you think other immigrants have problems like this? What do you think would be the most difficult adjustment going to another country where the culture is so different?

In the second narrative, an immigrant talks about the "rules of adaptation." What do you think he means? Why is this so important to him? Why do you think he is so concerned with finding a job and contributing to American society? Do you believe, as he does, that following his "rules" will keep him from having bad experiences here?

What similarities and differences do you see in the stories?

In Their Own Words

Seeta Chaganti, whose parents emigrated from India, describes their early life in the U.S.

The Kindness of Strangers

Because my father and mother did not come to this country from India together, their first memories of arriving here differ. But those vivid initial impressions have profoundly affected their feelings about both America itself and their lives as Americans.

When my father's plane landed in Boston in 1960, he realized that the 10,000-mile journey from southern India to New England had been less difficult than the journey ahead of him: the one from the airport to his dormitory room at Harvard, where he was going to study biology. The thick Boston accent of the friendly airport guard confused him when he asked for directions. In the subway station, he didn't know what tokens were, and had to ask another helpful stranger. And when he finally did find his dorm room, the roommate who awaited him kept a cat skull and a gun, wandered naked around the suite while preparing for bed, and generally unnerved my father to the point where he felt unable to share a bedroom with the peculiar philosophy graduate student. My father spent his first night in America curled on the red vinyl cushion of a living room window seat, staring into the darkness.

Three days later, the wife of my father's professor was the first person who thought to ask what he'd been eating since he arrived. When he revealed that, unable to find vegetarian meals, he'd been living on apples, she kindly explained the graduate student cafeteria. My father's professor showed no such interest in his cultural adjustment. He sat my father down, thumbed through a course catalogue, told him which courses he would be taking, and showed him out of the office in 15 minutes. And that was the beginning of my father's life in this country.

In 1970, my mother arrived in New York City with my father and me, then three years old, and she remembers holding my hand fairly constantly during her first several weeks here — out of fear for herself or for me, she wasn't sure. The policemen near the West Side grocery stores terrified her with their guns and their uniforms. In those first few days, the enormous quantities of food that she saw piled up in shops, on vendors' carts, and in restaurants nauseated her and emphasized the uniquely lonely feeling of being in a foreign land. In India, she had never done any cooking, and now she had to enter the overwhelming grocery stores, navigate the looming pyramids of fruit and the confusing array of boxed instant rice, and even try to find the spices and *dahls* that would remind her of home. And always, she was surrounded by crowds of people whose racial and ethnic diversity were unlike anything she had ever seen at home. In the beginning, they made her feel bewildered and isolated. She missed her affectionate family, and knew, as she sent those first letters home when she arrived here, that it would be a month or more before she received responses from India, which seemed to recede further and further from her.

In Their Own Words

Now, my parents look back and see in those first anxious days in America some of the things they have grown to admire most about this country. The multiracial population once so foreign to my mother has shown her America's capacity for accepting its newcomers. She is now a true New Yorker who revels in her city's variety of peoples and cultures. And while her separation from her family saddened and frightened her at first, both she and her family are proud of the home and career she has made in this country. My father finds in America a unique blending of personal independence and generous compassion. From that first interview with his professor, he was always treated just like any other student; judged for his abilities, not his foreign background; and expected to sink or swim. At the same time, even after years in what many deem the planet's unfriendliest city, he has a strong faith in the kindness of strangers, established by those first sympathetic few who helped him on his way.

An Immigrant from India

The following statement was written by Lester Joseph D'Costa, who now lives in Madison, Wisconsin.

I am an immigrant born in the city of Nagpur (state of Maharashtra) with ancestral ties to [the state of] Goa, India.

After working for a few years in the shipyard, I was given the opportunity to follow my brothers who had earlier migrated to this country.

My initial expectations were to (a) adapt to the situation, in terms of climate, culture, etc. (b) better my prospects of finding a job and putting my skills to use and (c) contribute my share to this society and [at the] same time be an asset to the working force.

I have not had any negative experiences, the reason being that adaptations to situations as mentioned above are very important.

I strongly believe that this country has a lot to offer to anyone, provided the individual can prove that he or she will be an asset to the working force, and thus all of them can continue to make this a great country.

We Change — Traditions Remain

Traditions, whether music for the ear, food for the body, or stories for the soul, are called folkways. Folkways are important expressions of every culture and nation. Folkways keep heritage and history alive. They are bridges from one generation to the next. For immigrants, folkways are bridges to their homeland; links to the memories, people, and traditions of the past. Folkways carry on the traditions of a people from one generation to the next.

The traditions and culture of India, Pakistan, and the Middle East cannot be separated from the rich religious heritage of their people. Art, music, theatre, literature, and even foods are influenced by the world views of Hinduism, Sikhism, Islam, Judaism, and Christianity.

Jerusalem, for example, is the spiritual heart of Christianity, Judaism, and Islam. The Wailing Wall is a site of Jewish prayer while nearby, Muslims pray at the Dome of the Rock, and Christians celebrate communion at the Church of the Holy Sepulcher. Religious art and expression is everywhere.

In Muslim nations in the Middle East, artwork often takes the form of geometric shapes and vibrant colors. People are not often portrayed because some Muslims interpret the Koran (the holy book of the Islamic religion) to say that human portraits are a form of idolatry, or worship of false gods. Some Christians, including the Amish, have the same belief.

Songs and poetry are often on religious themes. Although there are many wonderful folktales from Arab culture, including *One Thousand and One Arabian Nights*, religious themes and characters are frequently found in folktales as well.

Indian art often portrays Hindu gods as well as themes from nature and folklore. Tales of the Hindu gods Krishna and Kali are common. Other folktales show British influences, from the centuries when England traded with and later ruled India.

Some folkways show the influence of Islamic Bedouin culture, although part of that culture is disappearing. Bedouins move from place to place, following food and water or grazing lands for their animals. When "home" is a tent and people are on the move, crafts and musical instruments have to be portable. A loom can be easily dismantled. A potter's wheel or forge cannot. For that reason, perhaps, weaving cloth and rugs became a common creative expression in the Middle East.

In cities and towns, artisans create pounded brass, blown glass, and tile for mosaics. These arts are used to make places of worship beautiful.

South Asia and the Middle East are, to a great extent, cultures formed around the cornerstone of religious faith. You may learn much about the spiritual interests and motivations of human beings as you learn about the traditions and folkways of the people of South Asia and the Middle East.

Folkways in a Nation of Immigrants

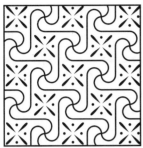

The following projects will help you learn about the traditions and folkways of immigrants from South Asia and the Middle East. Learning and enjoying the art, food, stories, music, drama, and crafts of other cultures is like opening a window into the history and heritage of other people. You will experience traditions still practiced in South Asia and the Middle East today. And you will learn to appreciate traditions practiced by your neighbors and fellow Americans.

- Prepare the recipe for hummus, a food from the Middle East, that is found in this unit. Or find another recipe for a food from India, Pakistan, or a Middle Eastern country. Prepare the dish to share with the class.

- Find out about one of the following writers: Kahlil Gibran, Georges Shehade, Michel Chiha. Tell your class about the writer you chose. Read one of his works aloud.

- Find a store that sells rugs made in the Middle East. Trace or copy patterns from the rugs. Duplicate the colors in these rugs in art pencil, oil pastels, or watercolor. Share your creation with your class.

- The Koran, the Muslim holy book, forbids creating idols in human form. Some Muslims take this to mean that all drawings, sculptures, or artistic representations of humans are not allowed. So Middle Eastern art uses geometric and natural patterns instead. Find pictures or illustrations of any of the following Middle Eastern art to bring to class: mosaics; stained glass or blown glass; wood inlaid furniture, trays, or artwork; hammered brass; silk brocade; woven rugs.

- Using cloth or paper, copy a Middle Eastern mosaic. Are there any shapes, patterns, or colors that are common in these mosaics? Find out common uses for mosaics in art or architecture. Tell what you learn and show your project to the class.

- Find hammered brass from India, Pakistan, or the Middle East. Copy the intricate patterns by placing a sheet of paper on the brass and rubbing the paper with charcoal or a pencil. Bring rubbings from as many hammered brass items as you can find. Shop owners may be willing to allow you to make rubbings from items if you ask.

- Folktales in the Middle East and South Asia often use religious characters or themes. Find such a folktale from one country to learn and tell to your class.

- The tales of *One Thousand and One Arabian Nights* are famous throughout the world. Read some of the stories. Tell one to your class.

- Find the Indian stories of Rama and Krishna. There are many versions. Read or tell one aloud to your class or write the stories in your own words.

- Learn the story of Muhammad's life. Who was he? Why are his writings important? Tell the story to your class. Read some examples of Muhammad's writings aloud.

- Find tapes or CDs of Middle Eastern or Indian music to share with the class. Learn about the musical scale used in the Middle East. Tell your class about what you learn.

Folkways in a Nation of Immigrants

❦ Find examples of poetry from Arab culture. Read a poem aloud to your class.

❦ Find out how Arabic calligraphy is done. Practice making some of the letters using a calligraphy pen and ink or a felt pen with calligraphy-type tip. Show examples to the class. Also, bring in examples of Arabic calligraphy from books, magazines, or on-line sources.

❦ Collect pictures from India, Pakistan, or Arab countries in the Middle East. Make a collage to show the diversity of this region. Show clothing; hair styling; skin color; facial features; and accessories such as jewelry, henna decorations, or headcoverings.

Folkways in a Nation of Immigrants

Hummus

INGREDIENTS

½ jar tahini sauce

1 can chickpeas

water

1 teaspoon garlic powder

juice of one medium lemon

cumin powder

salt

ground black pepper

olive oil

paprika

(OPTIONAL):

pine nuts

fresh parley

chopped fresh tomatoes

chopped fresh cilantro

1. Put the tahini sauce in a large bowl. Add water a little at a time, and mix with a mixer or by hand. Be careful not to add too much water at once, or the water won't mix well with the tahini sauce. Keep adding water until the mixture is smooth and thicker than soup. You'll know you've added enough water when the mixture changes from brown to a whitish color. You will end up adding about the same amount of water as tahini sauce.

2. Mash the chickpeas with a fork, a potato masher, or an electric food chopper. You can mash them as much as you like. (Some people like to have pieces of chickpea in their hummus; others like it to be completely smooth.) When the chickpeas are mashed, add them to the tahini and water mixture.

3. Add garlic powder to taste. (You can add more than 1 teaspoon if you'd like!) Then gradually add the lemon juice. Be careful to add just enough lemon juice to get the texture and consistency you want; if you add too much, it could be too watery.

4. Add a little cumin powder, then a little black pepper and salt.

5. Mix it all together, and serve.

To serve:

Spoon the hummus onto a plate. With a large spoon, make a well or hole in the middle of the hummus. Pour a puddle of olive oil into the hole. Sprinkle a little paprika on top, You can also add pine nuts, chopped fresh parsley, chopped fresh tomatoes, and/or chopped cilantro, if you'd like.

Scoop onto pita bread and enjoy!

Research & Writing Topics

The following list includes suggestions for individual or group research and writing projects for this unit on immigrants from South Asia & the Middle East

❦ Choose a fiction book about life in South Asia or the Middle East, or about the lives of immigrants to America from either region. Write a report about the story and its meaning to you. Summarize your report orally to the class.

❦ Trace a large map of the Middle East, including India, Pakistan, and surrounding nations. Using magazines, photocopied pictures from library and reference books, and on-line graphics, find illustrations of as many cultural/ethnic groups in this region as possible. Look especially for pictures of national costumes, traditions, or cultural lifestyles. Attach pictures to show where people live. Write captions under your photos giving information about each ethnic group, its people, traditions, and unique ways.

❦ Some Middle Eastern immigrants came to the United States in the mid- to late 1800s. Many were Lebanese. Find out about these immigrants. Where did they settle? Why did they come? What jobs did they do? What impact did they have upon society? Write a report about what you learn.

❦ Choose one nation from this unit. Find a famous person from this ethnic group who has contributed to American society in some way. Write a report about his or her life, experience, and contributions.

❦ Choose one of these political events to research. Find out what happened, how the Middle East, Pakistan, or India was affected, and how immigration was affected. Write a report about what you learn:

    Turkish oppression of Armenians in the 19th century
    Indian resistance to and liberation from British colonial rule
    Establishment and international recognition of Israel
    Arab-Israeli wars between 1948 and 1973
    Settlement of the West Bank by Israel
    The Iranian revolution
    The Lebanese Civil War
    The Persian Gulf War
    Resettlement of the West Bank by Palestinians

❦ Learn about the caste system in India. How does it work? Does it still have a role in Indian society? Has the caste system affected immigration to the United States? Write a report about what you learn.

❦ What were the Camp David Peace Accords? Find out about these historic meetings between Egyptian and Israeli representatives and President Jimmy Carter. How did these meetings affect relationships among countries in the Middle East? Write a report about what you learn.

❦ How was the nation of Israel established after World War Two? Find out about Zionism in Europe and the U.S. While many immigrants have come to the U.S. from other Middle Eastern countries, what has the history of immigration been between Israel and the U.S.? Write a report about what you learn.

Research & Writing Topics

South Asia & the Middle East

🕮 Learn about one of the following groups of people or organizations: Mahatma Gandhi, Indira Gandhi, Jawaharl Nehru, Yassir Arafat, the PLO, Gamal Abdel Nasser, Anwar Sadat, Menachem Begin, Yitzhak Rabin, Golda Meir, the Ayatollah Khomeni, Saddam Hussein. How did they contribute to or affect the United States and other Middle Eastern and South Asian nations? How did they affect international politics and the internal government of their nation or region? Write a report about what you learn.

🕮 Find out about the historical beginning of Islam, Christianity, Judaism, or Hinduism. Learn where and in what ethnic culture each religion began. What are the fundamental beliefs of people of this faith? Interview a person who practices this religion. Consider how this religion affects the people, traditions, and government in South Asia or Middle Eastern countries. Write a report about what you learn.

🕮 Learn about India's drive for independence from Britain. How did it occur? Why was it important? How did it affect emigration? Write a report about what you learn.

🕮 Interview someone from India or the Middle East who lives in your city or town. Learn about the people in your region who share this ethnic background. Find out why, how, where, and when this person's own family came to the United States. Ask about this person's traditions from and ties with his or her family's homeland. Ask this person why he or she thinks people from that country immigrated to the U.S. Write a report about what you learn.

Eastern Europe

NOTE TO TEACHERS:
The materials on the
student pages that
follow are intended to
provide your students
with background,
project ideas, and
topics for research.
You may choose to
share some or all of
these pages directly
with your students. Or
you may choose to
adapt and format
them to fit your own
schedule, curriculum,
and philosophy.

This unit on Eastern Europe focuses on the nations once known as the Soviet Union, or USSR; Poland; Czechoslovakia; Hungary; and the Balkan States. It also focuses on Jewish immigrants, who came largely from Russia and Poland.

The history of immigration to the United States from this region is a history of war, violence, poverty, and political oppression. In the 1800s, Polish immigrants fled poverty and a system in which only a few people owned land and rented it to many others. Immigrants from Russia and the Ukraine fled religious persecution and an oppressive feudal system that kept the poor in poverty and preserved the wealth of the rich.

Russians fled pogroms, "re-education camps," and communism's ever-tightening hold on intellectual, political, and economic freedom. Stories abound of refugees hiding in fishing boats, walking hundreds of miles at night, and hiking across mountain ranges to freedom.

You must decide how much weight to give the Holocaust and immigration related to World War Two in this unit study, as well as in your study of Western Europe. Other units specifically on this subject may have sufficiently covered this and related material. However, the impact of war and genocide on immigration to the United States cannot be ignored.

Many films address the Holocaust and immigration related to the Nazi threat to Jews in both Eastern and Western Europe. Careful prescreening of such films is necessary to evaluate content.

The following ideas would enhance and further develop this unit:

❦ Invite a Holocaust survivor to speak to the class.

❦ Invite members of local associations of Poles, Russians, Lithuanians, Hungarians, Czechs, Slavs, Slovaks, or members of another Eastern European ethnic group, to address the class. Ask them to bring in samples of folk crafts, music, or dance. If they are immigrants, ask them to tell the story of how they came to this country.

❦ Ask students whose own ethnic background is Eastern European to interview their parents and grandparents about when, where, why, and how their families immigrated to the U.S.

❦ Read aloud from the writings of Alexander Solzhenitsyn or Elie Wiesel.

❦ Have the class study the poem inscribed on the base of the Statue of Liberty.

❦ Set aside a single time for students to share food, crafts, and projects from the We Change — Traditions Remain and Folkways in a Nation of Immigrants portions of this unit.

Why They Came to America

The following is a brief history of the people who came to the United States from Eastern Europe — Russia; Hungary; Czechoslovakia; Poland; Croatia, Serbia, and Yugoslavia (the Balkans); and Estonia, Lithuania, and Latvia (the Baltics). In addition, this section covers the Jewish migration — which particularly involved Jews from Eastern Europe.

JEWISH IMMIGRANTS Jewish immigrants to America did not come from one country, but from many. The great majority of Jews who moved to America came from Eastern Europe.

In 1654, the first Jewish immigrants to the United States arrived in what is now New York City. Jewish immigrants played a significant role in the American Revolution and in helping establish the U.S. government after the war was over. The Jewish population in the U.S. remained low, however. Then from 1882 until the beginning of World War One, more than two million Jews came from Russia, what is now Poland, and other parts of Eastern Europe to settle in America. They came here to escape poverty and oppression. The governments of Austria-Hungary and Germany had political parties whose ideas were based on anti-Semitism, or hatred of the Jews. At the same time, Russia had laws specifically designed to oppress Jews, and they were the victims of pogroms, or organized mob violence. More than 75 percent of the Jews who emigrated were fleeing pogroms. Jewish immigrants from Europe stopped first in New York City. Many stayed there, on New York's Lower East Side. Others left for other urban centers.

In the 1920s, immigration in general was virtually ended in the United States. As Adolf Hitler and his Nazi regime rose to power, the Nazis began to systematically persecute the Jews. But even in the face of this persecution, few German Jews were allowed into the United States. Nazi persecution would lead in World War Two to the Holocaust, during which six million European Jews were put to death.

The nation of Israel was established in 1948 as a homeland for the Jewish people. Many Jews from around the world moved there. However, outside of Israel, the United States remains the country with the largest Jewish population.

RUSSIA In the 1800s, there were scattered Russian settlements on the West Coast and elsewhere in the United States. Then, in 1867, the United States purchased the territory of Alaska from Russia, making the many Russians who lived in Alaska at the time subject to our nation's laws. Many of these Alaskans gave up their Russian citizenship and became Americans. The greatest influx of Russian immigration began in 1880. Many of these immigrants were Jews. Others were Russian German farmers who followed the Mennonite religion. They settled in the Great Plains and brought a hardy wheat — red bulgur — with them. This wheat is now a staple agricultural product in our nation.

More Russians came here after the Bolshevik Revolution in 1917 and the communist takeover in 1918. Many of them belonged to the nobility who were fleeing the new communist rulers in their native land. Russian immigration between the years 1924 and 1976 was minimal. During that time, Russia was

Why They Came to America

the leading country of the Soviet Union, a group of nations with communist governments. The Soviet Union and the United States were enemies, except during World War Two, when they were allied against Hitler's Germany. After World War Two, the U.S. and the Soviet Union were especially hostile to each other. In 1976, more than 100,000 Russian Jews were allowed to leave the Soviet Union, where they faced discrimination. Most of these Russian Jews moved to Israel, but about 10 percent of them entered the United States. With the collapse of the Soviet Union in 1991, more than 20,000 Russians have moved to the United States each year. Today, more than four million people of Russian heritage live in the U.S.

HUNGARY The number of Hungarian immigrants who came to this country between 1870 and 1920 is not known. For most of these years, what is now Hungary was part of other countries, including Austria and Russia. The closest count shows that between half a million and two million Hungarian immigrants came to America in those years. Hungarians came here because of war and persecution in their own land. The immigrants who came here were a diverse cross-section of society. They included nobility, highly-trained professionals, scientists, and laborers.

In 1956, about 200,000 Hungarians came to the U.S. as refugees. At that time, the Hungarian government had tried to get more freedom from the Soviet Union, which had ruled Hungary since World War Two. The Soviets repressed any attempt at freedom by any country in their bloc, and some Hungarians revolted. The revolution was crushed and Hungarian refugees fled abroad. Most of them came to the U.S.

CZECHOSLOVAKIA Prior to 1920, when Czechoslovakia became an independent country, Czech immigrants to America were classified as Austro-Hungarians. It is estimated that perhaps 500,000 people of Czech descent came to America before 1920. Most of them traveled here in the last quarter of the 19th century to escape religious and political persecution. Many of the Czechs who came here were miners or farmers, although many others settled in large urban centers in the Midwest and Southwest. Today, there are an estimated two million people of Czech heritage in the U.S.

POLAND Between five and 13 million people in the United States have some Polish ancestry. People of Polish descent represent one of the largest ethnic groups in this country. Polish immigrants first came here in 1609, landing in Jamestown, Virginia. But it wasn't until 1795 that Polish people began coming here in great numbers. At that time, their country ceased to exist; it was taken over by Austria, Prussia, and Russia. By the time of the Civil War, there were an estimated 30,000 Polish immigrants living here. After 1870, a huge number of poor Polish immigrants streamed to the U.S. It is estimated that about two million Poles — often listed as other nationalities — came here between 1870 and 1900. Many of these immigrants were Jews. Others were Catholic and Protestant. But all were fleeing the almost

Why They Came to America

constant struggle among other nations to control their native land. Poland became an independent country in 1920, only to be overrun by Germany in 1939 and by the Soviet Union after World War Two. It was not until the collapse of the Soviet Union in the early 1990s that Poland again became independent.

Most — but not all — of the Poles who moved here were very poor. They were laborers, miners, and farmers who settled throughout the country.

THE BALKAN STATES The Balkan States of Croatia, Serbia, and Yugoslavia have historically been dominated by other countries. They were part of the Turkish Ottoman empire in the 19th century, and then part of the Austro-Hungarian empire until 1918. From 1920 until 1940, the nation of Yugoslavia was an independent state. By that time, about 700,000 immigrants from the Balkan region had come to the U.S. When Yugoslavia got its independence, 30 percent of these people moved back to their homeland. During World War Two, the Balkans were taken over by Germany. After World War Two, the countries were ruled by communist regimes (although they were not part of the Soviet Union).

Immigrants from this area were often counted as Austrians when they first moved here in the latter part of the 19th century, so an accurate count of their numbers here does not exist. They came to escape the repressive regimes that dominated the Balkan countries, and to flee ethnic warfare among groups in their countries. Most of them settled in industrial centers where they worked in steel mills and other factory environments.

THE BALTIC STATES The Baltic states of Latvia, Lithuania, and Estonia have been ruled at various times by Denmark, Sweden, Poland, and Germany. In the 19th century, they were controlled by Russia's czar. When the Bolshevik Revolution took place in 1917, the countries became independent. But in 1940, the Soviet Union seized the countries, and they didn't regain their independence until 1992, when the Soviet Union crumbled. The tiny nations have always been sought after by their neighbors because they border the Baltic Sea and have important harbors. Through it all, the countries have retained their own distinct cultures.

By 1885, more than 15,000 Lithuanians had left their country for America. A few years later, their numbers had swelled to more than 300,000. Immigration from Latvia has been smaller, but still significant. An estimated 5,000 Latvians moved here in 1908 following an attempted revolution in their country. They were followed by 30,000 more in the first two decades of the 20th century. Today, there are an estimated 1.5 million Americans of Lithuanian descent here, and an estimated 300,000 Americans of Latvian descent. Estonian immigration has been smaller still, with an estimated 100,000 Americans of Estonian descent in the U.S. today.

In Their Own Words

NOTE TO TEACHERS:

The following material relates the experiences of some Eastern European immigrants to America. The material includes a cartoon from the beginning of the century about immigration and the personal testimonies of a first-generation Jewish woman, a Polish immigrant, and a worker in the sweatshops of New York. Some possible topics of discussion include:

The cartoon shows former immigrants opposing the movement here of other immigrants. It appeared during a time when millions of Eastern Europeans moved to America. What is the point of the cartoon? Is the cartoon pro- or anti-immigration, or is it anti-hypocrisy? Does this cartoon reflect American attitudes toward immigrants today?

In the first interview, Molly Laitman says that although Jews were ghettoized on the East Side of New York, and she is sure there was prejudice against Jews, she remembers being happy because of the community around her. What role does community have in helping people become acclimated to a new land?

The letter from the Polish immigrant discusses some possible disadvantages of community. Discuss these disadvantages. On the whole, does a community of immigrants help the individual in a new country? What role does assimilation play in making an immigrant an "American"? Is assimilation good or bad?

The material about working in a sweatshop seems to be typical of the experience of many immigrants from this time. That is, immigrants were often exploited and had to work in jobs that others would not take. Do you think this experience is still true today? Why or why not?

In Their Own Words

LOOKING BACKWARD
THEY WOULD CLOSE TO THE NEW-COMER THE PATH THAT CARRIED THEM AND THEIR FATHERS OVER

Cartoon from the early 1900s

In Their Own Words

**Interview with
Molly Laitman,
age 88**

Living on the Lower East Side

My mother and father were married in what was at that time Russia, then it became Poland. And they were married in a city that was called Kamenitz. My father left my mother to come to what they called in Yiddish the *Goldene Medina*: the gold world. He wanted to make sure that he could shovel up some gold before he brought my mother here. There was unrest in Russia at that time. The Cossacks came and the Jewish people were hated, and they had to go into cellars where [the Cossacks] couldn't reach them. They came through, the Cossacks, and they raped the women and they shot everybody. So it was time to move on. My mother had three sisters there with children and grandchildren. They all went to the ovens [in Nazi concentration camps during World War Two]. The only one that came was Tante Ruchel. She got married here in the United States.

So [my father] came in 1900. He left his wife and two sons. By 1905, he was working very hard. And he told my mother, "It's time to come." So she packed up. In those days, the treasures were a down comforter and brass candlesticks. Those were the two items that were the most that people treasured. And they came [here in] steerage. [This meant they traveled in a ship, packed in "steerage" class with many other poor immigrants. Steerage was crowded and uncomfortable.] It took them two weeks to get here. And when she came, the world was not paved with gold. She worked very hard to maintain the family that she had. And then her first born here was in 1906. I came later. I came in 1908. The Jewish people that came were all ghettoized. They came to the East Side [of New York City]. And there all the Jews were together.

[My parents] had a hard life coming here. But they didn't have any pogroms and they didn't rape the women, and it was a little easier. They were ghettoized and so long as they spoke Yiddish and Russian and Polish, all the other people did the same thing. It was hard to come into a new language. [But] I don't think that they were aware of [any prejudice] because they stuck close to their own people. But there was prejudice. Yeah, there was prejudice. The Jewish people were hated. And they lived a, like a ghettoized life. And they were kinda happy. They didn't have beautiful homes, they didn't have all the luxuries that people have today.

My sister was born on the East Side. So was I born on East 11th Street. So in order to have some money, [my mother] would take in the people that came from Europe and maintain a boarder house. Besides, my father was making maybe ten dollars a week in those days. But she had to put up these people who came. And they were called *landsleit*. That's people that came from the same area that she came from. She took care of them. She cooked for them, she washed their clothes, and that was her way of adding to whatever money was coming in.

In Their Own Words

Now when I was born, my sister was two years old. And I remember that my mother used to put me on the fire escape 'cause she had no time to take me out for a walk to get fresh air. Below me, below where my mother lived, was a family that had a parrot. And this parrot would talk to me. They were one floor below. And he would talk and I would answer. And I got my first words from the parrot. And I continued being on the fire escape until I was able to walk. I couldn't walk then. I was a baby.

My father worked for my uncle. And he had a big — not a chain, but he did very well. He delivered coal. My father worked for him and he delivered coal and all kinds of material that the stove required. There was no steam heat in those days, [it] was coal operated. So that was the beginning of [the] United States, and it didn't take long when they felt the pavement was not paved in gold. You had to work for it. But they were ghettoized, and we lived on the East Side. I know my brothers graduated public school on the East Side and then high school, so we were there for a long time. My oldest brother, when he graduated he had to go to work. My brother Dave wanted to go to college. So they sent him to Pace Institute where the boys learned accountancy. He was very good at that. My brother Sol was a salesman and he used to bring all the money to my mother. We used to do that, too. When I went to work, whatever I earned, I took five dollars for fare and lunches, but the rest was [for] my mother. She took care of the money.

We didn't stay on the East Side too long, and then we came to Brooklyn. And we had a four room apartment and we were four children. And we had an apartment opposite a park. So when it got really warm, my father used to take us to the park and we'd sleep in the park overnight. And if it started to rain, everybody got a cover and we ran for shelter. But that was the beginning. And we thought that this was a country life. Was no longer a city life. And my father went into business for himself where he was selling seltzer, bottled seltzer and beer. And he had a horse and wagon. He was brought up on a farm and he loved animals. So when he went into business he couldn't drive a car, so he got a horse and wagon and there was a stable close to where we lived, he kept his horse there, and when the horse got sick he used to stay with the horse all night. And so it went. We got older, we got a little smarter, we didn't speak Russian or Polish, but we spoke Yiddish, and we spoke the other language here, and we grew up.

In Their Own Words

Letter of an Anonymous Polish Immigrant

"If you can help me ..."

I'm in this country four months (from 14 Mai 1913 ...).

I am polish man. I want be american citizen — and took here first paper in 12 June N 625. But my friends are polish people — I must live with them — I work in the shoes-shop with polish people — I stay all the time with them — at home — in the shop — anywhere.

I want live with american people, but I do not know anybody of american. I go 4 times to teacher and must pay $2 weekly. I wanted take board in english house, but I could not, for I earn only $5 or 6 in a week, and when I pay teacher $2, I have only $4 — $3 — and now english board house is too dear for me. Better job to get is very hard for me, because I do not speak well english and I cannot understand what they say to me. The teacher teach me — but when I come home — I must speak polish and in the shop also. In this way I can live in your country many years — like my friends — and never speak — write well english — and never be good american citizen. I know here many persons, they live here 10 or more years, and they are not citizens, they don't speak well english, they don't know geography and history of this country, they don't know constitution of America. — nothing. I don't like be like them I wanted they help me in english — they could not — because they knew nothing. I want go from them away. But where? Not in the country, because I want go in the city, free evening schools and lern. I'm looking for help. If somebody could give me another job between american people, help me live with them and lern english — and could tell me the best way how I can fast lern — it would be very, very good for me. Perhaps you have somebody, here he could help me?

If you can help me, I please you.

I wrote this letter by myself and I know no good — but I hope you will understand whate I mean.

> Excuse me,
> F. N.

Report of the Commission on Immigration on the Problem of Immigration in Massachusetts, 1914.

In Their Own Words

A New York Sweatshop

Russian Jews who immigrated to New York often took jobs in garment factories in lower Manhattan. Harry Roskolenko was only five when he saw his first sweatshop. His father worked at a pressing machine.

When I arrived at the factory there he was, my father, soaking wet with sweat. It was just an ordinary shop, I discovered, with nothing special about the men, the work, the heat, the dirt, the pay, the boss, the production. It was a factory with a hundred workers stripped down to their pants. All sorts of tailoring, cutting, and pressing machines were whirling, whirring and steaming away. I was fascinated for a few minutes — then I saw my father. I lost the magic of a new place at once. The inventions were gone — and there was a man of fifty, pressing a cloak with a ten-pound steam iron.

... A few pigeons would reach the fire escapes for the bits of stale bread that a worker had put there — for a moment of flight and magic. The pigeons would make off, when the steam blew their way. Instead of fans there were foremen walking about, fuming and blowing, their voices like dogs barking at other dogs.

The workers seldom paused, no matter what they were at. They talked every language but English; and the foreman, when queried over some confusion in the work, answered in every language. When the foreman laughed, everybody laughed — machinelike, blending with the pigeons, the smells, and the steam, into one great bubble of gas. After the laugh — back; the moment gone, allowed, created by some eccentricity on the part of the foreman. It had likely cost the whole factory a dollar in production. ...

They were producing winter wear, heavy coats and cloaks, in the summertime. Outside, the temperature was almost 100 degrees. Indoors, it rose to 110 or 120 — humid, steamy, all-encasing, gluey. At the tables they got so much per garment pressed or so much for sewing on sleeves, collars, linings, bodies — whatever went to make up the finished garment. It was so little usually and the cause of many strikes and sudden stoppages. With this system of sweating, every worker gave up his lunchtime — the minutes saved, to earn a bit more. Eat faster or eat less. Or eat what took up no time at all — and then back to the steam and the machines, and to the *gontser macher* barking to his dogs.

Harry Roskolenko, *The Time That Was Then* (New York: Dial, 1971), quoted in Milton Meltzer, ed., *The Jewish Americans: A History in Their Own Words*, 1650-1950 (New York: Thomas Y. Crowell, 1982).

We Change — Traditions Remain

Traditions, whether music for the ear, food for the body, or stories for the soul, are called folkways. Folkways are important expressions of every culture and nation. Folkways keep heritage and history alive. They are bridges from one generation to the next. For immigrants, folkways are bridges to their homeland; links to the memories, people, and traditions of the past. Folkways carry on the traditions of a people from one generation to the next.

By the mid-1800s, when immigrants from Eastern Europe came to America in great numbers, Eastern Europeans already knew about and shared parts of their different cultures. A traveler could begin in Siberia, tour Poland, Germany, Hungary, and the Ukraine and find similarities in the folkways of the people. Woodcarving, painting, embroidery, and tinwork are common folk arts in nearly every country. The figures, colors, and images used in Ukrainian folk art may be quite similar to the art in Moravia or Poland.

While the food, culture, music, and folkways of Eastern European countries are similar, it would be a mistake to think that they melt together or are identical. People have a strong sense of national and ethnic identity, and differences in the style, colors, and techniques of the folk arts are important to the people.

One example is the tradition of painting and dyeing eggs. In the Ukraine, Lithuania, and Moravia, detailed patterns are sketched on eggs with wax. Then artists create beautiful multicolored patterns by dyeing unwaxed areas, removing the wax, and creating new designs. Artists in each country use this technique. The patterns are similar, and include religious and traditional symbols. However, knowledgeable people would know the difference between an egg done by a Ukrainian artist and one from Lithuania. Tiny differences in style are valued because they reflect the pride of national and ethnic identity.

Folk arts in Eastern Europe reflect the geography and natural surroundings of the region. These forested regions produce wood for carving and flax for weaving. Sheep in that cold climate produce wool for embroidery and needlework. Even the folklore centers on farmland, mountains, and forests.

The history of war and conflict has influenced folkways in Eastern Europe. For centuries, large nations have attempted to swallow smaller ones. The same ethnic groups that were controlled by the Austro-Hungarian empire were later under the thumb of Germans and, later still, part of the Soviet Union. Some folklorists think this history has affected the way folk traditions have developed in smaller countries. Some traditions were simply swallowed up by traditions from larger countries.

One example of this is the experience of Mennonite refugees. Mennonites fled religious persecution in Moravia and Germany. Some fled to Holland or Switzerland. Some fled to Russia, where they were accepted for their skill as farmers. Later, when persecution again drove the Mennonites from their

We Change — Traditions Remain

homes, they sought safety and religious tolerance in the United States, Canada, and Paraguay. Today, American Mennonite cookbooks include Russian blini and borscht alongside beef-stuffed pastries from Paraguay. Women learned needlework patterns from Germany, Switzerland, and Russia. These patterns show up today in Amish and Mennonite quilts in America.

People change, but traditions remain. Even today, Eastern Europeans come to America looking for opportunity, freedom, or a new life. Even today, they bring traditions with them — stories, foods, and crafts that are symbols of heritage, history, and national pride.

Folkways in a Nation of Immigrants

The following projects will help you learn about the traditions and folkways of Eastern European immigrants. Learning and enjoying the art, food, stories, music, drama, and crafts of other cultures is like opening a window into the history and heritage of other people. You will experience traditions still practiced in Eastern Europe today. And you will learn to appreciate traditions practiced by your neighbors and fellow Americans.

❧ Prepare the recipe for matzoh balls, an Eastern European Jewish food, found in this unit. Or find and prepare a recipe from any Eastern European country. Share the food with your class. What do you notice about Eastern European food that's different from other types of food?

❧ Learn about *psanky*, traditional egg dyeing done in the Ukraine, Czechoslovakia, Lithuania, and the Czech region of Moravia. In these four areas, patterns and methods of making these traditional Easter decorations are similar. Find out how these eggs are made. Using patterns, you can make *psanky* yourself. Although artists in Eastern Europe use special tools for putting melted beeswax on eggs to create patterns, beeswax can be applied with toothpicks. Read about *psanky* to learn what the patterns symbolize. Show your project to the class and tell about the symbols. Traditional equipment for making *psanky* is available from the Ukrainian Gift Shop, 2422 Central Avenue NE, Minneapolis, Minnesota 55418. **NOTE: Be careful! The hot wax can burn. Make sure you get your teacher's okay before you begin this project. Teachers or parents should be on hand to supervise. You can melt beeswax safely in a large can placed inside a pot of boiling water. Weight the can with stones if necessary.**

❧ Use traditional, natural materials to dye eggs. Eastern Europeans use walnut hulls for brown color; onion skin, lilac flowers, and bark of a wild apple tree for yellows; berries (raspberries or cranberries) for red; blueberries for blue; and sunflower seeds cooked with the berries of elder trees for green. You may think of other natural ways to create colored dyes. Experiment with blown or whole eggs to see how natural materials can create color.

❧ Braided Easter bread is a traditional food throughout Eastern Europe. Find out how it is made and make some to bring in to class. Why are eggs used? What do they symbolize?

❧ Pounded tin artwork is common in Eastern Europe. Research to find some common patterns and symbols used in tin work. Using a hammer, nail, and large tin can, make a lantern using patterns and designs you find. **NOTE: do this project only under teacher or parent supervision.**

❧ Some Eastern Europeans, especially the Moravians, decorated beehives, wine presses, and cookie molds with wood carvings. Find out about these decorative carvings. Whenever possible, find photos or drawings. Bring in examples to the class.

❧ Polish children played with "saint dolls" created with salt dough to portray people honored by the Catholic church. Salt dough figures of characters from traditional folktales were also used as toys. Find instructions for making salt dough. Then, using characters from folklore, create your own story figures. Bake and paint or varnish the salt dough. Use the figurines to tell the story to a younger class or preschool group.

Folkways in a Nation of Immigrants

🐦 Find a folktale from any Eastern European country. Learn and tell the story to a younger class.

🐦 Find a folktale from each of five different Eastern European countries. Compare the styles, themes, and characters. How are the stories similar? How are they different?

🐦 Baba Yaga is a traditional Russian folk figure. Find a Baba Yaga story. Bring it in to share with the class.

🐦 Isaac Bashevis Singer was a well-known Jewish writer and storyteller from Poland. Read any story by Singer aloud to the class.

🐦 Many children's books tell the story of Peter and the Wolf. Find one of these books. Find a copy of the symphony *Peter and the Wolf* by Sergei Prokofiev. Do you think the music does a good job of telling the story? Why or why not? How do you think the story and the music complement each other? Share the story and the symphony in class.

Matzoh Balls

This food is often served during the Jewish holiday Passover

Enjoy with soup or alone!

INGREDIENTS

4 eggs

matzoh meal

water

salt

pepper

1. Break 4 eggs into a large bowl. Add a half-eggshell of water for each egg (4 half-shells in all). Add a little salt and pepper. Beat the eggs and water up well.

2. Pour matzoh meal into the bowl until the batter is thick and heavy, not liquidy. Let the batter sit for about 20-30 minutes, until it sops in the matzoh meal and the mixture gets really heavy, not loose.

3. Boil water in a large pot. Add salt and pepper to the water. Stir the batter again, so everything gets mixed up.

4. Fill a small bowl with cold water, and place it next to you while you work. Form the batter into balls using your fingers and a large spoon. Dip your fingers in the cold water to help keep the batter from sticking to your hands.

5. When the water in the pot has reached a full boil, throw your matzoh balls into the pot. Let the boiling water turn the matzoh balls. The rolling action of the water will help the matzoh balls hold together. Let the balls boil in the water until they hold together but they're still fluffy — about 25-30 minutes. *Carefully* take them out of the boiling water with a slotted spoon.

Makes 8-9 matzoh balls

Research & Writing Topics

The following list includes suggestions for individual or group research and writing projects for this unit on immigrants from Eastern Europe

❦ Choose a fictional account of life in Poland, Czechoslovakia, Hungary, Russia, the Ukraine, or any other country in this area, or a book about immigrants to America from this region. Write a report about the story and its meaning to you. Present the report orally to the class.

❦ Trace a large map of Eastern Europe as the countries are today. Using magazines, photocopied pictures from reference books, and computer graphics, find illustrations of as many cultural/ethnic groups in this region as possible. Look especially for pictures of national costumes, traditions, or cultural lifestyles. Attach pictures to show where the people live. Write captions under your photos giving information about the ethnic group, its people, traditions, history, and unique ways.

❦ Learn how and why people left the Soviet Union from the 1940s to 1990s. Write a report about this subject. Find two interesting true stories to share with your class.

❦ Mennonites from the Ukraine immigrated to the United States in the 1870s. They left the Ukraine and settled in the Kansas Territory for very specific reasons. Find out why. What was their life like in Europe? What was it like here? What did they bring to the U.S. that was of great value?

❦ What are pogroms? Learn why Jews emigrated from Russia to the U.S. Where did they settle? Why?

❦ Learn about the present-day Jewish community of Crown Heights, New York. Who lives there? Why? Where did residents of this community come from? Write a report about what you learn to share with the class.

❦ Learn about the serf system in Russia. Many people emigrated from Russia during the time the serf system was in place. Do you think the serf system influenced immigration? Why? How? Write a report including your own reflections.

❦ Choose one of the following people to research and write about. Learn where this person came from, what his or her life was like, and why he or she is or was important in that nation's history:
   Joseph Stalin, V.I. Lenin, Leon Trotsky, Pope John Paul II, Alexander Solzhenitsyn, Lech Walesa, Nikita Krushchev, Vaclav Havel, Alexander Dubcek, Boris Yeltsin, Leo Tolstoy, Antonin Dvorak, Jan Hus, Isaac Bashevis Singer, Emma Goldman

❦ When the Soviet Union controlled many smaller nations, old disagreements seemed to disappear among these countries and ethnic groups. But when the USSR broke apart, the old hatreds and problems came to life again. And some parts of the Soviet Union tried to break away from Russian control. Research the history of the breakup of the Soviet Union. Did it lead to ethnic conflicts? Did the breakup affect immigration to the United States?

Research & Writing Topics

Eastern Europe

❧ Although the Soviet Union did not control it, Yugoslavia also had a communist government for many years. After the death of its leader, communism fell apart and old disagreements again appeared. Research the history of the Bosnian conflict. Learn how it started and what the problems are now. Write a report on what you learn. Consider how disagreements and ethnic hatred, both in the past and present, might influence people's decisions to leave their homeland to settle in America.

❧ Read a fiction or nonfiction book about the life of Jewish immigrants in New York City during the late 1800s and early 1900s. What made their experience and life unique? Write a book report.

❧ Learn about the shipyard and mining strikes in Poland during the 1970s and '80s. Why were these important? How did they change Poland's government?

❧ Read one fiction or nonfiction book about World War Two, Nazism, or the Holocaust. Write a report about this book and its meaning to you.

❧ Find out about Raoul Wallenberg. Who was he? What did he do? Why is he a hero? Write about what you learn and share it with the class.

❧ Once, Russians spoke of being "sent to Siberia." What did they mean? Learn about how the communist government used prisons, secret police, and the government-controlled press to rule the Soviet Union. Did their efforts work? Why or why not? Write a report stating what you learned and your own thoughts on the topic.

❧ In 1889, Jane Addams and Ellen Gates Starr founded Hull House in Chicago. Hull House was a settlement house. Its purpose was to help poor people, many of them new immigrants from Eastern Europe. How did Hull House help immigrants? What did it do to make life better for the poor of Chicago? Find out more about settlement houses. What was their purpose? Were they successful in their stated goals? Do they still exist today in some form?

Western Europe

This unit on Western Europe focuses on immigrants from Ireland, Scandinavia, Italy, Greece, France, Spain, Portugal, Germany, Austria, the Netherlands, and England. Because of their heritage or personal interest, some students may wish to research topics or folkways from other Western European countries. Some projects may be flexible enough to accommodate this.

The time frame of Western European immigration is the largest of any immigrant group. From the first waves of English investor-driven settlement and French fur traders in the early 1600s until the flight from Italian fascism or Nazi persecution in the mid-1900s, Western Europeans have sought new homes in America. Western Europeans have, through the years, made up a huge number of immigrants to America. In 1910, for instance, nearly 10 percent of all American citizens had Irish parents.

The Western European immigrants had tremendous influence in populating our cities and settling the American West. Many well-written fiction books are available that tell personal stories of Western European immigrants.

The following ideas would enhance and further develop this unit:

- An all-class project about quilt making might enhance the study of folk traditions within the English and Scandinavian immigrant communities, especially. Quilt patterns are included in this unit. One class project suggestion is to distribute quilt patterns to students and cover up the pattern names. Ask students to think of a name for the pattern and write a story about why they think the pattern should have this name. Then, using either fabric scraps or paper, have students create quilt squares in their chosen patterns. Assemble squares on a large sheet of colored paper. Students can write the actual name of the quilt pattern below their square. The students' stories and the names they invent may be displayed around their quilt. Other suggestions for activities with the quilt patterns can be found in the Folkways section of this unit.

- Set aside a single time for students to share food, crafts, and projects from the We Change — Traditions Remain and Folkways in a Nation of Immigrants portions of this unit. Tapes or CDs of Irish folk songs or Swedish fiddle music would make a nice background.

- If musicians from a Western European background live in your area, invite them to share their music or dance with your class.

- Contact an area knitters' guild or yarn shop to meet knitters skilled in Irish or Norwegian knitting. Invite them to bring in samples and demonstrate knitting to your class.

❧ Contact area high schools to find out whether any exchange students from Western Europe are attending nearby schools this year. Invite them to share knowledge about their homeland with your class.

❧ Ask if any students of Western European background have relatives who immigrated to the U.S. Invite them to tell the class about their experience as immigrants. Or have students interview relatives who know the story of their family's immigration.

Why They Came to America

The following is a brief history of the immigrant groups that came here in large numbers from Western Europe. The countries featured in this section are England, Ireland, Germany, Austria, the Netherlands, the Scandinavian countries, Italy, Spain, Portugal, France, and Greece. Although immigrants did come from other places in Western Europe, this unit focuses on these areas because this is where most immigrants came from.

ENGLAND Most of the earliest settlers in North America came from England. They settled on the Eastern seaboard, from north to south. These immigrants came to America to forge a new way of life. Some, like the Pilgrims, wanted religious freedom; others wanted the opportunities the new land offered, and still others came to escape imprisonment. The first U.S. census in 1790 said that 78 percent of the 2.75 million people living here were of British birth or ancestry. There is hardly an area of our present way of life that has not been touched by the immigrants from England. The earliest English settlers gave the country its language, many of its customs, and, eventually, its legal system and way of government. Between 1820 and today, more than five million more English citizens have immigrated. Today, 14 percent of the U.S. population traces its heritage to Great Britain.

IRELAND The Irish didn't begin their mass migration to the United States until the 1840s, although the first U.S. census in 1790 counted 200,000 people of Irish descent in this country. Between 1820 and 1840, another 700,000 Irish immigrants came to America. In the decade following 1845, millions of people left Ireland. Many of them came to America. Most of them were very poor. The main reason so many people left Ireland was a disease that struck the potato crop, the food most people in Ireland depended on to live. Nearly one million people starved because of the famine brought on by the failure of the potato crop. And between 1846 and 1860, nearly two million Irish immigrants made it to America. Thousands of Irish immigrants came to America every year up until 1930. For the most part, they settled in the large urban centers of the East, gradually moving west. Because they had been poverty-stricken farmers, most of them had little or no money to start a new life in America. Many of them settled in the poorest areas of a city and took any job they could get. The men took laboring jobs and the women became maids and housekeepers. From the beginning, the new Irish immigrants took an interest in politics, especially on the local level. They saw politics as a way to help get themselves out of their desperate poverty. Many large cities soon had Irish political "machines"— that is, organized groups of politicians supported by the votes of their numerous Irish constituents. Today, an estimated 14 million people in the U.S. claim some Irish ancestry.

GERMANY German immigration to the U.S. began early. The 1790 census counted more than 200,000 German immigrants, or about 10 percent of the U.S. population. The Napoleonic Wars, fought from 1803 to 1815, brought many more German immigrants here. And between 1820 and 1900, nearly five million Germans came to the United States. Today in the U.S., close to 35 million people claim some German heritage. That means more people in this country have some German ancestry than any other background. Many German immigrants came here to escape poverty and political upheaval. Others came to escape religious persecution. In the middle part of the 19th century, Germany was not one country. It was divided into a number of smaller countries and even large landholdings. In the 1850s, the often-bloody

Why They Came to America

process of unifying Germany into one country began. In addition, Germany fought wars with Austria and France to get more territory. By 1871, Germany was a unified country. But by this time, many Germans had left the war-torn area for the United States. Many of the new immigrants were farmers, and others were artisans and craftspeople.

AUSTRIA The true number of Austrian immigrants to the United States is not known. At one time, the Austro-Hungarian empire consisted of Bohemia, Moravia, Galicia, Serbia, Bosnia, Hungary, and Austria itself. When people from these countries came here, they were all classified as Austrians by the Bureau of Immigration, even though they came from many different countries and had different ethnic and cultural heritages. Between 1901 and 1910, more than 2.1 million citizens from the Austro-Hungarian Empire came to the U.S. More than half a million more followed in the decade from 1910 to 1920. Most of them were poor, landless farmers who sought to gain economic relief and escape from a strict government. Others fled at the beginning of World War One.

THE NETHERLANDS People from the Netherlands were among the very first European settlers in the New World that would become the United States. They came in the wake of Dutch explorer Henry Hudson's trip up the river that bears his name. They colonized New Amsterdam — now New York City — in 1625. Most of these early Dutch settlers were fur traders, although settlers began farming the New Amsterdam area in 1640. Many present-day names in the New York area are derived from the original Dutch names. They include Brooklyn (Breucken), Harlem (Niew Haarlem), and Flushing (Vliesingen). A second wave of Dutch immigrants came in the 1800s, escaping the Napoleonic Wars that put their country under French rule. Only about 400,000 Dutch immigrants came to this country between 1820 and 1970.

SCANDINAVIA The Scandinavian countries are Norway, Sweden, and Denmark. Of these countries, Sweden has sent the most immigrants to the U.S. Today, about 12 million Americans have some Swedish ancestry. In the years between 1870 and 1920, more than a million Swedish immigrants came to America. They came to escape poverty and hunger in Sweden, which had gone through a period of crop failures and massive unemployment. So many farmers and lumberjacks emigrated from Sweden to the U.S. that they are credited with clearing and plowing more acres in America than there are in all of Sweden. The peak period for Swedish immigrants to America was from 1875 to 1890.

Like the Swedes, most of the Norwegian settlers to the United States had close ties to the land. They began coming to America in the 1840s, and their numbers rose throughout the 19th century and into the early 20th century. By 1910, about 800,000 Norwegians had made America their home.

Many of the Danish immigrants to America also were farmers. By 1920, about 350,000 Danish citizens had moved to America. American citizenship was also extended to the 3,500 Danes living in the Danish West Indies when the U.S. purchased those islands in 1917 and renamed them the Virgin Islands.

Why They Came to America

ITALY   In 1850, there were about 5,000 Italian immigrants in the United States. By 1900, that number had swelled to more than 500,000. And between 1901 and 1910, more than two million Italians came here. The majority of the Italian immigrants were poor, uneducated people from Southern Italy. For decades they had lived with political instability and the numerous battles that were fought to unite Italy as one nation. Natural disasters such as floods, earthquakes, volcanoes, and plant diseases also made life miserable for many Italian citizens. And Italian peasants suffered under a system that did not allow them to own land and made them the heavily-taxed tenants of rich landowners and the nobility. When they came to America, Italian immigrants settled in the poorest parts of the nation's biggest cities. They began as unskilled laborers and farmers but soon became prominent in all the professions. Today, more than 23 million Americans have some Italian heritage.

SPAIN AND PORTUGAL   The actual Spanish immigrants who came here were, and are, few. While those with Spanish heritage in this country number in the millions, almost all of them came from Mexico and the other countries of Latin America. People with heritage from the country of Spain itself number under a half million in the United States. But the Spanish influence on America is immense. Spanish forces founded the first permanent European colony here in 1565 at St. Augustine, Florida. Between 1540 and 1565, the Spanish introduced horses, cattle, sheep, and pigs to North America.

About 500,000 Portuguese immigrants have come to America since its discovery by European explorers. They settled mostly on the Eastern seaboard. Many people with Portuguese heritage are farmers and fishermen.

FRANCE   The French were among the earliest explorers and settlers in the New World. Many of the early immigrants settled in the southeastern part of the United States, around Florida and South Carolina. These settlements failed. Others settled around Louisiana, establishing New Orleans. Thousands of French people came to America after 1685, when religious persecution drove them to the New World. But the greatest number of French came to this country to work in the fur trade. The first European exploration of the area around the Great Lakes and down the Mississippi River was done by French missionaries and traders. Just before the Revolutionary War, in what is known as the French and Indian War, the English colonies fought the French for control of upper North America. This war was an extension of a conflict between France and England in Europe. The English (and American) colonists won, and put an end to French colonization in America. However, the French still had strongholds in Canada, and today, the Canadian province of Quebec is a center of French culture. In 1803, the United States purchased Louisiana and a huge territory beyond it from Emperor Napoleon of France, making French settlers in the area American citizens. Today, about three million people in the U.S. claim some French heritage.

Why They Came to America

GREECE Greek immigration to the U.S. didn't begin on a large scale until the 1890s. Over the next 30 years, nearly 400,000 Greek immigrants settled here. They came because of political oppression, poverty brought on by crop failures, and the desire to make enough money here to return home and start a family. Like many other immigrants, most of these early settlers never returned to their homeland. Instead, they brought their families over here. From 1920 to 1960, quotas kept Greek immigration low. But after 1965, immigration picked up again. Today, an estimated three million people claim some Greek heritage.

In Their Own Words

NOTE TO TEACHERS:

In this section, immigrants to the U.S. tell about their experiences coming to and living in America. Along with a letter written by a German immigrant, we have included an article that shows the condescending attitude many American citizens had toward immigrants. We have also reprinted an anti-Irish cartoon from the middle of the 19th century.

Some possible points of discussion:

This cartoon was drawn by Thomas Nast, a well-known political cartoonist of the 19th century. What is the point of the cartoon? What stereotypes can you identify in the cartoon? Why do you think there was so much anti-Irish feeling at the time this cartoon was first published in the middle of the 19th century? Do you see any similarities or differences between the feelings about immigrants expressed here and the feelings about immigrants today?

In "What of the Italian Immigrant?" the writer supports immigration, but still shows that he is prejudiced. What is the point of the article? How does the writer exhibit his feelings and prejudices? What do you think of the article? How would you respond to this article if you were an Italian immigrant?

The letter included here was written by a German woman in the 1850s. The story of her life in America is fairly typical of the life faced by those immigrants who became farmers here. What differences and similarities do you see in her life and the life of a farmer today? How do you think the community of German immigrants helped newer settlers?

Drawn in the 1860s by Thomas Nast

In Their Own Words

What of the Italian Immigrant?

No serious student of history or of natural conditions can doubt but that this influx to our shores of the foreign element has been of vast material and national advantage and has permitted America to assume its present position in the affairs of the world. And it were well to-day, now that conditions are changed and the cry of "Put up the bars and shut out the immigrants," is heard on all sides, for our people to consider the history of our past in the light of the labor and achievements of our foreign-born citizens; for any legislation aimed at general exclusion of foreign immigrants in the future would necessarily prove a terrible blow to our national life and to the prosperity and advancement of our people.

While the old-time necessity for immigration no longer exists, it is idle to claim that there is no room, work or opportunity for those who seek our shores in search of a new fatherland. Indeed, there are many occupations that the native American refuses to follow, but for which many foreigners show great aptitude. Wise and equitable immigration laws are assuredly

In Their Own Words

required, for the time has come when certain restrictions are just and necessary. ... It might also seem wise to enact laws against foreigners who come to our shores only temporarily, having no intention of remaining and becoming citizens, for those thus coming have no real interest in our country or love for our institutions and traditions, and America calls to-day more than ever before for citizens whose first and only allegiance and love are for our common country. There should also, I think, be a certain educational test and qualification; but beyond such amendments to our present immigration laws no barriers should be raised.

It is not enough, however, to welcome the right kind of immigrants to our shores. Wise and far-seeing statesmanship no less than high humanitarian considerations call for the adoption of sane and practical measures which promise as rapidly as possible to transform these penniless immigrants into thrifty, wealth-producing and independent American citizens. The congestion of the foreign element in our largest cities is perhaps the most serious feature of the immigration problem to-day. ... I feel that a discussion in which I shall be able to give the actual experience in relieving urban congestion, in so far as it relates to the Italians, may be valuable as indicating how the problem of the superfluous foreign population can be partially if not chiefly solved. ...

It was evident that the greatest danger to our entire citizenship, and the greatest curse to our Italian population, lay in the fearful crowding and congesting of the Italians in the cities of our country, where like flocks of sheep they had the poorest of homes and the smallest of chances to succeed in life and become law-respecting and intelligent citizens. ...

My work among the Italians has shown me that while they are as a race simple-minded and often grossly ignorant, still they are quick and eager to learn and are thankful to be permitted to take their place as free men with a common country. While over-suspicious, as is always the case with a people that has been crushed down and oppressed for generations and kept in ignorance and poverty, they are, when once their faith and confidence are gained, trustful and faithful to those whom they believe to be their friends. ... [T]he Italians are above all agriculturists and tillers of the soil. This fact ... suggests the solution of the problem, which is to get the Italians away from the cities and out into the country and onto the land.

Folger Barker, "What of the Italian Immigrant?" *Arena* 34,(August, 1905).

In Their Own Words

Among the hundreds of thousands of Germans who immigrated to the Midwest were Christiane Barck, her husband Edward, and August and Sophie Frank. In 1850, they left Dietlingen, Baden, and bought farmland near the Titibawassee River in Saginaw County, Michigan, where a sizable number of Germans already lived.

Christiane Barck to Her Parents in Germany

Titibawassee, March 8 [1852]

It is so silent around me, not even a mouse is stirring. August and Henry are hauling hay from the stack into the barn because it is raining today and the stack has been started already. Barck is not quite well and is lying in bed, Sophie is visiting Madame Lisko, who is ill. And last, the dear little ones are with their uncles, and are trampling down hay in the barn. They are permitted to take turns driving, which makes them so jolly that I can hear them laughing and hollering here in the house. The dishes are washed, the room is swept and I have a few free hours until time for the cooking of the evening meal. Mr. Seyffardt bought a farm and is living on it now, but visits us on Sundays. In the meantime Barck has shot a deer again. The more he shoots, the more he loses the buck-fever. We have no news from Ernst from New York and are worried about it. We will start making sugar this week, since it is getting milder. The snow is melting. There must be clear days and cold nights when one wants to make sugar. The men have cut about 10 cords of wood and a big kettle will be walled in with bricks. This will save a lot of wood and makes cleaner sugar. Henry works with untiring diligence and is strong and healthy in spite of his long stay in Africa's unhealthy climate. This week one of the cows will have a calf, and we will have butter and milk again. It is a rather hungry life, not having milk for one's coffee. If our German acquaintances would have not been so good as to supply us with milk, I would be desperate for I have become a real coffee-fiend, and cannot drink it black. Please, dear Mimi, send me the recipe for hare's-ear. We could make it here because we often have venison. It should keep for a good quarter year. We prepare venison in three ways. When fresh, we have beef steaks, which are delicious. Then depending upon the pieces, we have sauerbraten and pepper, and from the lungs and liver, liver dumplings. Now the hens are beginning to lay, so we have had as many as twenty eggs. This makes Sophie very happy. You can imagine that we were sometimes irked when we had to make pancakes and dumplings without eggs and milk, but it did not seem to bother the men when they came home from the woods and fell to over the filled dishes. One is in America and gets used to everything. You would laugh if you would see our large bowls, but it is always better to pay for food than to give it to the doctor, which is a big expense here. We are well supplied with doctors. A very skilled one named Blessner from Prussia is in Saginaw, and last summer one came whose name was Frank. There are a few English doctors, but the Germans never go to them because they usually do not understand anything. The Scheuermanns will be starting out soon and will be here the middle of May. That will make a hustle and bustle on our farm next spring. If Binder leaves for Germany we will send you a sample of our sugar. Oh, if you could be here at sugar-making time. What a nice thing it is and how one can lick. Dear Mathilde should be here, for she has such a sweet tooth, as I remember from old times. Farewell all, all you dear ones!

In Harry H. Anderson, ed., *German-American Pioneers in Wisconsin and Michigan: The Frank-Kerler Letters, 1849-1864* (Milwaukee, Wis.: Milwaukee County Historical Society, 1971).

We Change — Traditions Remain

Traditions, whether music for the ear, food for the body, or stories for the soul, are called folkways. Folkways are important expressions of every culture and nation. Folkways keep heritage and history alive. They are bridges from one generation to the next. For immigrants, folkways are bridges to their homeland; links to the memories, people, and traditions of the past. Folkways carry on the traditions of a people from one generation to the next.

Western Europe stretches from the glaciers of northern Scandinavia to the sunny hill country and fishing villages of southern France and Spain. Because individual countries are as small and close together as our states in the U.S., some Americans think the cultures in Western European countries are also similar. That is not always so.

In this unit, your study will focus on only a few of the immigrant groups from Western Europe. By learning mainly about the traditions and folkways of immigrants from Scandinavia, France, Germany, England, Italy, and Ireland we leave out the many people who came from other Western European countries. Each group has unique folkways worth learning about.

The traditions, foods, music, art, and dance of Western Europe were packed into the hearts and minds of immigrants as carefully as winter clothing was packed into steamer trunks bound for America. Once immigrants settled in the United States, traditions and folkways were sometimes the only link between life in America and life back home. Those links were precious to people who knew they might never see friends or family again.

Think of a French voyageur camped by a river in Minnesota, singing folk songs and telling tall tales. Imagine a Norwegian woman carefully saving paper to cut delicate star-shaped decorations for her windows because they reminded her of Christmas at home. Think of Irish immigrants so poor they took boarders into their own two-room New York apartment in order to pay the rent. Yet, they still gathered to sing Irish folk songs and dance.

Some traditions and folk arts reflect the role of women in Western Europe. For example, beautiful needlework done in England and France was a creative outlet for bored, wealthy women in the 1800s, when physical work was done only by poor women. The bright colors and flower patterns common to painting and needlework in Scandinavia may have reflected ways women tried to brighten the darkness of the long northern winters. The beautiful patterns of Irish and Norwegian knitting showed how women turned practical, necessary work into an art form.

Western Europeans have kept many of their folkways and traditions. Swedes still hold midsummer festivals and dance to fiddle music. Irish folk music has become popular across the U.S. Traditional needlework skills transformed into the beautiful art of American quilt making.

Enjoy creating and learning about the folkways and traditions of Western European immigrants.

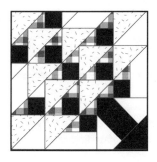

Folkways in a Nation of Immigrants

The following projects will help you learn about the traditions and folkways of Western European immigrants. Learning and enjoying the art, food, stories, music, drama, and crafts of other cultures is like opening a window into the history and heritage of other people. You will experience traditions still practiced in Western Europe today. And you will learn to appreciate traditions practiced by your neighbors and fellow Americans.

- Bake Irish soda bread using the recipe found in this unit. Find out about St. Patrick's Day traditions that are celebrated in Ireland and in your city or region. Finally, find out what the Irish in Chicago do to the Chicago River on this holiday. Tell your class what you learn.

- Find out about traditional foods in one Western European country. Prepare a dish and share it with the class. Tell where it came from and describe any traditions that go with this food (for example, Swedish heart-shaped pancakes served on holidays, regional foods in France or Italy, etc.).

- Your teacher has some traditional quilt patterns. Pick one pattern and write a story about how the pattern you picked got its name. Recreate the pattern using paper and glue or cloth. Try to create your own pattern. What would you call it? Why?

- Make a traditional Swedish papercutting. A pattern is available from your teacher.

- Find, trace, and color traditional Norwegian rosemaling patterns. You may use oil pastels, colored pencils, paints, or crayons. Find out about the colors common to rosemaling. Show your project to the class.

- Learn about Irish folk music. Some instruments are unique; learn what they are and how they are played. Find tapes or CDs to share when you tell your class what you learned.

- Learn about Punch and Judy puppet shows, which originated in Italy, but which combine elements from Italy, France, and England. Write a puppet script of your own to perform for a class of younger children. If this is a group project, you can make your puppets out of papier-mâché for a more accurate show.

- Find a folktale from Ireland, England, France, Italy, or Scandinavia. Learn it by heart and tell it to your class.

- Irish folklore is famous for its leprechauns and little people. Find an Irish tale about these creatures and tell it in your own words, either aloud or in writing.

- Tomtens, ogres, gnomes, and dwarves "live" in the folklore of Scandinavia. Find a story either about gnomes or about the Tomten. Tell, read, or write this story for your class.

- Learn about the minuet, a traditional French dance. Ask a dance teacher to show you the basic steps to the minuet and demonstrate it for the class.

- Learn a Paul Bunyan tall tale to read or tell to your class. Be sure to explain to the class where the Bunyan tall tales come from, and who invented them.

Folkways in a Nation of Immigrants

🎵 Bring in a video or audio tape of an Italian opera. Tell the story of the opera to your class, in your own words. Read about an Italian opera or a famous opera singer and tell your class what you learn in writing or out loud.

🎵 Read or retell the folktale of Romulus and Remus aloud to the class.

🎵 Roman, Greek, and Norse mythology are ancient sources of legend and folklore. Find a Greek, Norse, or Roman myth to tell in your own words.

🎵 Read one of the many stories about King Arthur or Robin Hood. These heroes of English folklore may have been real people who, like Paul Bunyan, became bigger than life. Tell the story in your own words.

🎵 Homesteaders had a hard life. Read *Little House on the Prairie*, by Laura Ingalls Wilder, to learn how a log cabin was built. Her description is detailed and interesting. Use her directions to build a diorama showing a homestead and log cabin. Logs may be constructed from salt dough, formed and baked to shape, or from actual sticks, carved to fit together. Think creatively about how to show life on the prairie. Some students may even build a prairie by filling a low box made of plywood with a plastic-lined bottom with potting soil. Grass seeds planted in the soil will actually grow to form a miniature prairie. Also, think of creative ways to depict a sod-construction barn, split-wood fences, stone or stick and clay fireplace, well, or cleared fields. Show this project to your class. Do research about the lives of homesteaders and explain to your class how homesteaders used what they found and grew to survive.

🎵 Settlers in Jamestown, one of the first English settlements in America, made the mistake of choosing a mosquito-infested area to live in. They built their homes using a method called "daub and wattle." Learn how these houses were built. Make a model of a daub and wattle house. Modeling clay can be used as a base. Sticks and pliable willow branches, like those actually used for this building method, can be used to "weave" walls. You can think creatively about ways to show the bundled-straw or thatched roof and mud-plastered walls. Find out what happened to Jamestown and report what you learn to the class.

Folkways in a Nation of Immigrants

Irish Soda Bread

Irish soda bread is baked in many homes throughout Ireland. This recipe uses regular flour to make white soda bread, although wheat flour can be used to make a brown loaf.

Preheat the oven to 375° F.

INGREDIENTS

6 cups white flour

1 cup buttermilk, fresh milk (add 1 teaspoon cream of tartar to dry ingredients if using fresh milk), or sour milk

1 teaspoon baking soda

1 teaspoon salt

1. Mix all the dry ingredients together in a bowl and make a well in the center. Add enough milk to make a thick dough. Pour the milk in large quantities. Stir with a wooden spoon. Mix lightly and quickly. Add a little more milk if it seems too stiff.

2. With floured hands, put the mixture onto a lightly floured board or table and flatten the dough into a circle about 1½ inches thick. Put the mixture onto a baking sheet and, using a floured knife, cut a large cross in the top of the mixture. (This ensures even distribution of heat.) Bake the mixture in the oven for about 40 minutes.

3. Test the center with a toothpick before removing from the oven. To keep the bread soft, wrap it in a clean dishtowel. Makes 1 large or 2 small loaves.

NOTE: To make brown soda bread, use the ingredients described above, but use 4 cups whole wheat flour and 2 cups white flour instead of 6 cups white flour. A little more milk may be needed to mix the dough.

For variety, add ½ cup sultanas (golden raisins) to the dough. To make treacle soda bread, heat 2 tablespoons black treacle (molasses) and add it to the milk, and add 1½ tablespoons sugar to the dough.

Folkways in a Nation of Immigrants

Birds of wood shavings, straw, and paper have long been common decorations in Sweden.

You will need:

1 — 8½" x 11" sheet of white paper

1 — 8½" x 5½" sheet of white paper

thicker paper or white cardboard for body

scissors

glue

Bird of White Paper

1. Fold the piece of thick paper or cardboard in half (Figure a). Cut out the bird from these instructions. Place the outline of the bird on the folded cardboard so the top of the bird is along the fold (Figure b). Trace the body of the bird onto the cardboard.

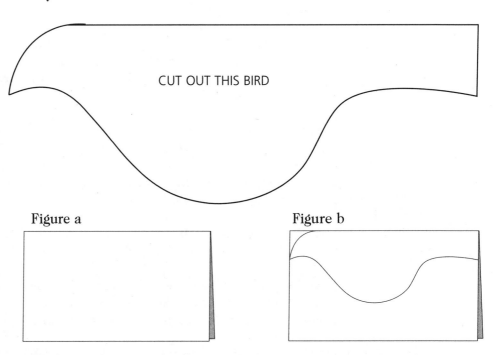

CUT OUT THIS BIRD

Figure a

Figure b

2. Cut out the bird's body along the outline. You should have a double-sided bird with a fold in the middle. (Figure c shows the bird's body unfolded.)

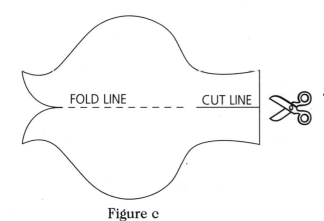

FOLD LINE ----- CUT LINE

Figure c

3. Cut the fold at the tail and glue the body together except for the tail. Press together and let dry. Cut a slot in the bird's back as shown.

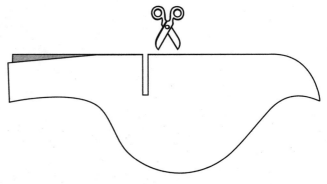

Folkways in a Nation of Immigrants

4. Beginning with the short side, fold the 8½" x 11" sheet of paper like a fan. Fold the 8½" x 5½" sheet the same way beginning with the long side.

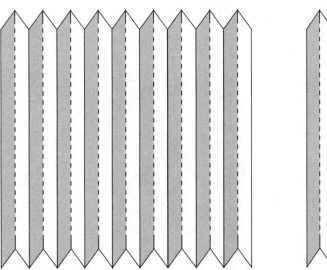 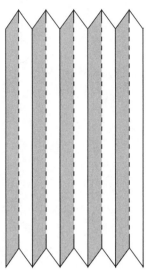

5. Cut patterns as shown on both sides of each folded piece of paper. The larger piece will be the wings. The smaller piece will be the tail.

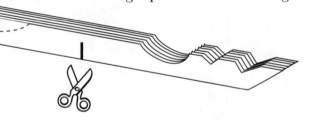

6. Attach and glue the wings in place in the slot in the bird's back. Fold the tail in the middle and glue into tail opening on both sides.

Folkways in a Nation of Immigrants

Quilt Patterns

Pick one pattern and write a story about how the pattern you picked got its name. Recreate the pattern using paper and glue or cloth. Now, create your own pattern. What would you call it? Why?

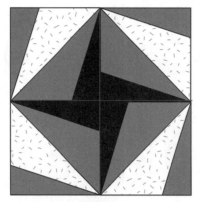

Perpetual Motion

True Lover's Knot

Chain and Bar

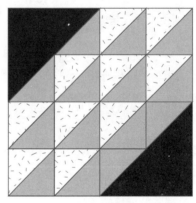

Migration

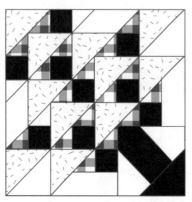

Apple Tree

Boston Belle

Research & Writing Topics

The following list includes suggestions for individual or group research and writing projects for this unit on immigrants from Western Europe.

❦ Choose a fiction or nonfiction book about the lives of people from Western Europe, either in their homeland or when they came to settle in the U.S. Write a book report telling about the story and its meaning to you.

❦ Trace a large map of Western Europe. Using magazines, photocopied pictures from library and reference books, and on-line graphics, find pictures of as many cultural/ethnic groups in Western Europe as possible. Look especially for illustrations of national costumes, traditions, or cultural lifestyles. Attach pictures to show where different groups of people live. Write captions under your photos giving information about each ethnic group, its people, traditions, and unique ways.

❦ Many famous music composers came from Western Europe. Find out about the life of one composer and write a report about what you learn. Bring in a record or tape of one piece of music composed by this person.

❦ Many famous artists came from Western Europe. Learn about one artist. Find a picture of a painting, print, bronze work, or sculpture by that artist. Write about the artist's life and work and show the picture to your class.

❦ Find out who Pierre Pauquette was and write about what you learn to share with your class.

❦ Find out about the fur trade that brought early French immigrants to America. Here are some topics to find out about:
   voyageur, portage, Jean Nicolet, Hudson Bay Company, trade goods, and voyageur's contracts.
Write a report about what you learn.

❦ Learn about the routes taken by fur traders. Trace them on a map. Find out all you can about how voyageurs lived every day. What did they wear and eat? How did they travel? What kind of contract did the Hudson Bay Company offer its workers? Write a report to tell what you learn.
(This idea can be combined with the previous suggestion for a good group project.)

❦ French Jesuit priests brought education, medical care, and religion to Native Americans in the northern U.S. particularly. Learn about Père Marquette, Father Joliet, or other Jesuit missionaries during the 1700s to mid-1800s. Write a report about what you learn.

❦ Which Western European people settled in your state? Contact your state historical society to learn about these people and where they settled. Choose one group to research and write about. Learn where they settled and when. Find out whether these people formed new towns and communities, settled in rural areas, or made their homes in the cities. What kind of work did they typically do? Finally, look on a map to find any cities and towns with names that may have come from Western Europe.

Research & Writing Topics

Western Europe

🐦 English people now called Pilgrims came to America seeking religious freedom. Many people mistakenly think all Pilgrims were alike. Find out for yourself! Find out about the Separatist Pilgrims and the Puritans. Learn why they left England and what kind of relationships they had with the Native Americans in the new land. Check a map to see where they settled. How were they similar? How were they different?

🐦 When and by whom was Jamestown settled? What happened to these settlers? Learn about the purpose of the settlement and write a report.

🐦 What was the Homestead Act? How did it affect people "back East"? What was the result of the Homestead Act for Native Americans? How did it affect immigration? How did a person file for and "earn" a homestead? Do an oral or written report on what you learn.

🐦 What was the Irish potato famine? Learn what happened and how it affected the lives of Irish people. Find out how it affected immigration to America. Write a report about what you learn.

🐦 Who are Cajun people? What is their cultural background? Learn about their culture, traditions, and language, and report to the class either orally or in writing.

🐦 What was the Louisiana Purchase? When did it happen? Why? How did it change America? Write about what you learn and share your information with the class.

🐦 What do you know about England? Millions of people left the British Isles for America between 1620 and 1890. They came seeking religious freedom and economic opportunity. First, trace and label a map of Great Britain. Choose one of the following groups and find out why, when, and where they came to America:

> Welsh miners, London factory workers, indentured servants, Irish farmers, and Quakers

🐦 Pennsylvania is called "Penn's Woods" for an interesting reason. Learn why William Penn and many thousands of other Quakers came to Pennsylvania from England.

🐦 Who was Napoleon? What did he do that changed the history of France? How did Napoleon affect America?

🐦 Why did Swedish and Norwegian farmers come to the U.S. by the millions between 1840 and 1890? Where did they settle and how did they live? Why do you think they chose this life? Find out the answers to these questions and write a report about what you learn.

Research & Writing Topics

Western Europe

- Many Germans came to America between 1830 and 1890. Why did so many German people come then? Contact your state or regional historical society. Learn about German immigration to your state. Where did Germans settle? Did they form new and separate towns and communities? Search your state map for towns and cities with German names. Compile a list and highlight the names to show your class. Write a report about everything you learn.

- By 1800, immigrants came to the United States on steamships from Europe. Learn about the experience of travelers, particularly the poor immigrants, on board these ships.

- Although Dutch and Spanish people didn't come to this country in great numbers, they influenced the course of the nation's history. Find out why the Dutch and Spanish first came here, where they settled, and why their influence diminished after the earliest days. Write a report and tell your class what you learn.

- What do you know about Ellis Island? Learn all you can about what it was, what happened to people there, and how people were evaluated to see if they would be allowed to enter the U.S. Find out what is carved on the base of the Statue of Liberty? Do you think the words there apply to America today? Think about why or why not. Write a report about what you learn. Read the words from the Statue of Liberty to the class and tell why you think they do or do not apply to today's America.

- Many immigrants settled in large cities in the East like New York and Boston. How did they live? Here are some topics to learn about:
  tenements, sweatshops, child labor, Children's Aid Society, Jacob Riis.
  Find out about life for poor immigrants in our nation's big cities.
  Write a report about what you learn.

- Learn about when and why people from Italy immigrated to America. Some were running away from war or political oppression. Others were desperately poor and hoped to make their fortunes in America. Where did Italians tend to settle in America? Write a report about what you learn.

- Do some research to find out about a famous person in your state or region from a Western European background. Write a report about this person's accomplishments and contributions.

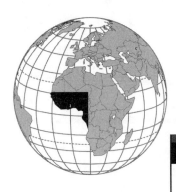

West Africa

This book contains information about immigrants from every corner of the globe. It includes people who immigrated to the United States as refugees fleeing war, in search of economic opportunity and land, or seeking political freedom.

The case of African immigrants is unique, however, because most African Americans did not immigrate voluntarily. They were kidnapped or sold by neighboring African tribes into slavery. Only after they won their freedom, by escaping to free territory or by legal emancipation after the Civil War, did African Americans have the opportunity to truly be immigrants — making new lives for themselves in American society and culture. Even then, their experience in America was tainted by the legacy of the slave system.

Most slaves were captured in West Africa. This unit will allow students to learn about the history of African immigration to and within the United States. The following ideas would enhance and further develop this unit study:

🐞 Invite a local expert in African American history to speak to students about the role your region, state, or town played in African American history. Perhaps you live in what was once a slave-holding state. Perhaps area people were abolitionists or active in the Underground Railroad. Perhaps your state or region was the site of black settlements and communities established either by escaped slaves or freedmen. Ask this scholar to tell true stories of black history that would be of interest to students.

🐞 Contact a local storyteller familiar with Anansi stories from Africa and the Americas or other African folktales. Ask this storyteller to visit your class.

🐞 Contact the National Park Service or your state historical society to find out about documented Underground Railroad or African American historical sites in your area. Arrange a field trip.

🐞 Read aloud the children's book *Wagon Wheels*, the story of Nicodemus, Kansas. This settlement was established by freed slaves after the Civil War. In spite of poverty, struggle, and crop failures, it grew into a vigorous community.

🐞 Ask your librarian for a tape or CD of African drumming or traditional African songs. Contemporary South African freedom songs may also be of interest. Play examples of this music for your class.

🐞 The office serving international students at your local university may refer you to students from Western Africa. Invite a student to share music, stories, dance, crafts, or other traditions with your class.

🐞 Set aside a single time for students to share food, crafts, and projects from the We Change — Traditions Remain and Folkways in a Nation of Immigrants portions of this unit.

NOTE TO TEACHERS:

The materials on the student pages that follow are intended to provide your students with background, project ideas, and topics for research. You may choose to share some or all of these pages directly with your students. Or you may choose to adapt and format them to fit your own schedule, curriculum, and philosophy. This unit also includes craft instructions that you can photocopy and distribute to your students.

Why They Came to America

This unit focuses on people who came to the United States from West Africa.

The ancestors of most African Americans are among the only immigrants to this country who came here against their will. They came here as slaves — as property owned by landowners who forced the slaves to work for them. Slaves had no rights. In most places, it was a crime for a slave to know how to read and write, their movements were severely restricted, and their families could be broken up at any time.

The majority of black Americans can trace their origins to an area in West Africa that was controlled by three empires — Ghana, Mali, and Songhai — from about 300 to 1500 AD. During the early 1500s, European nations began a slave trade in which blacks from West Africa were brought to the European colonies in the Americas.

Slavery was not a new idea for people in many parts of the world. Africa was no exception. Africans had enslaved other Africans since ancient times. In most cases, the slaves had been captured in war and sold to Arab traders in Northern Africa. But in the 1500s, the character and scope of the slave trade changed. Spain and Portugal became involved in the trade, followed in the 1600s by the Netherlands, England, and France. For the next 300 years, millions of Africans were forcibly shipped across the Atlantic Ocean to what are now Latin America, the Caribbean islands, and the United States.

The first blacks in the American colonies were brought in as indentured servants. That meant they had to work for a master without wages for four or seven years, and then they were freed. But soon after that, Africans were denied even these rights, and they were forced to work for their owners for life. By the early 1700s, more than 200,000 slaves lived in the colonies. Most of these slaves lived in the South, where the fertile soil supported large farms, or plantations, that grew rice, tobacco, sugar cane, and later on, cotton. The practice of kidnapping Africans and shipping them to America was banned in 1807, although the slave trade still thrived within the borders of the U.S. At the time of the ban, there were 700,000 slaves here; by 1860, there were four million.

After the Civil War, which was fought from 1861-1865 between the northern and southern United States, slaves were legally granted their freedom. At first, the former slaves had voting rights and other rights enjoyed by most other Americans. But soon, laws were passed that kept them from having the same rights as white people. These laws took away the right of most blacks to vote, and limited where they could eat, live, and go to school, among other things. Black Americans were also the victims of racism and prejudice. Many of the restrictive laws and the worst violence happened in the South, where most African Americans still lived. But unlike in slave days, African Americans could now move freely within the country. And many of them did. Between 1910 and 1920, a vast migration — the "Great Migration" — occurred, as African Americans left the rural South for southern cities. Soon they moved farther still, to northern cities like New York, Chicago, Detroit, and Los Angeles. This migration continued throughout the 1920s, but tapered off during the 1930s.

Why They Came to America

At that time, the nation was suffering through the terrible economic times called the Great Depression. After World War Two ended in 1945, the migration began again. African Americans were attracted by the large number of factory jobs in northern cities. They also hoped to escape some of the racism and discrimination they faced in the South. Unfortunately, many of them found that there was discrimination and prejudice in the North, as well.

Today, African Americans live in all parts of the country, although most live in larger cities. Their struggle for full economic and political equality goes on.

In Their Own Words

NOTE TO TEACHERS:

In this section, African Americans relate some of their experiences in slavery.

After reading these accounts, you might discuss with the class the role slavery played in America. Why was it so important to the South that it became one of the major reasons the Civil War was fought? Why was slavery not allowed in most places in the North in the early 19th century?

These excerpts will likely also spark discussion about how slaves were treated, and the conditions they were forced to live under. Why were slaves treated this way?

Another possible topic for discussion is the impact slavery had on the family life of the first African Americans who came here. Often, husbands and wives were kept apart. Any children they had were the property of the owner. How do you think this affected them?

How do you think the legacy of slavery affects the relations between white and black people today?

In Their Own Words

Olaudah Equiano — oo-LAW-dah eck-we-AH-no — was born in Biafra, in Africa, about 1745. After slave traders captured him, he was shipped to Barbados, Virginia, and England. He was renamed Gustavus Vassa. In 1766, Equiano bought his freedom. He spent the rest of his life working for the end of slavery.

Olaudah Equiano,
The Interesting Narrative of the Life of Olaudah Equiano, or Gustavus Vassa, the African, Written by Himself, 1789.

A Slave Describes His Capture

One day, when all our people were gone out to their works as usual and only I and my dear sister were left to mind the house, two men and a woman got over our walls, and in a moment seized us both, and without giving us time to cry out or make resistance they stopped our mouths and ran off with us into the nearest wood. Here they tied our hands and continued to carry us as far as they could till night came on, when we reached a small house where the robbers halted for refreshment. ... Thus I continued to travel, sometimes by land, sometimes by water, through different countries and various nations, till at the end of six or seven months after I had been kidnapped I arrived at the sea coast.

The first object which saluted my eyes when I arrived on the coast was the sea, and a slave ship which was then riding at anchor and waiting for its cargo. These filled me with astonishment, which was soon converted into terror when I was carried on board. ...

I now saw myself deprived of all chance of returning to my native country or even the least glimpse of hope considered as friendly; and I even wished for my former slavery in preference to my present situation, which was filled with horrors to every kind, still heightened by my ignorance of what I was to undergo. I was not long suffered to indulge my grief; I was soon put down under the decks, and there I received such a salutation in my nostrils as I had never experienced in my life: so that with the loathsomeness of the stench and crying together, I became so sick and low that I was not able to eat, nor had I the least desire to taste anything. I now wished for the last friend, death, to relieve me; but soon, to my grief, two of the white men offered me eatables, and on my refusing to eat, one of them held me fast by the hands and laid me across I think the windlass, and tied my feet while the other flogged me severely. ... [T]he crew used to watch us very closely who were not chained down to the decks, lest we should leap into the water: and I have seen some of these poor African prisoners most severely cut for attempting to do so, and hourly whipped for not eating. ... In this manner we continued to undergo more hardships than I can now relate ... [until] at last we came in sight of the island of Barbadoes.

In Their Own Words

A New Overseer

In this excerpt from his autobiography, ex-slave Frederick Douglass describes Austin Gore, an overseer at the plantation where Douglass lived.

Mr. Gore was proud, ambitious, and persevering. He was artful, cruel, and obdurate. He was just the man for such a place, and it was just the place for such a man. It afforded scope for the full exercise of all his powers, and he seemed to be perfectly at home in it. He was one of those who could torture the slightest look, word, or gesture, on the part of the slave, into impudence, and would treat it accordingly. There must be no answering back to him; no explanation was allowed a slave, showing himself to have been wrongfully accused. Mr. Gore acted fully up to the maxim laid down by slaveholders, — "It is better that a dozen slaves suffer under the lash, than that the overseer should be convicted, in the presence of the slaves, of having been at fault." ...

His savage barbarity was equalled only by the consummate coolness with which he committed the grossest and most savage deeds upon the slaves under his charge. Mr. Gore once undertook to whip one of Colonel Lloyd's slaves, by the name of Demby. He had given Demby but few stripes, when, to get rid of the scourging, he ran and plunged himself into a creek, and stood there at the depth of his shoulders, refusing to come out. Mr. Gore told him that he would give him three calls, and that, if he did not come out at the third call, he would shoot him. The first call was given. Demby made no response, but stood his ground. The second and third calls were given with the same result. Mr. Gore then, without consultation or deliberation with any one, not even giving Demby an additional call, raised his musket to his face, taking deadly aim at his standing victim, and in an instant poor Demby was no more. His mangled body sank out of sight, and blood and brains marked the water where he had stood.

A thrill of horror flashed through every soul upon the plantation, excepting Mr. Gore. He alone seemed cool and collected. He was asked by Colonel Lloyd and my old master, why he resorted to this extraordinary expedient. His reply was, (as well as I can remember,) that Demby had become unmanageable. ... He argued that if one slave refused to be corrected, and escaped with his life, the other slaves would soon copy the example; the result of which would be, the freedom of the slaves, and the enslavement of the whites. Mr. Gore's defense was satisfactory. He was continued in his station as overseer upon the home plantation. ... His horrid crime was not even submitted to judicial investigation.

Frederick Douglass, *Narrative of the Life of Frederick Douglass, An American Slave, Written by Himself* (Cambridge, Mass.: Harvard University Press, 1988), originally published in 1845.

In Their Own Words

The Life of a Field Hand

The principal food of those upon my master's plantation consisted of corn-meal, and salt herrings; to which was added in summer a little buttermilk, and the few vegetables which each might raise for himself and his family, on the little piece of ground which was assigned to him for the purpose, called a truck patch.

In ordinary times we had two regular meals in a day: — breakfast at twelve o'clock, after laboring from daylight, and supper when the work of the remainder of the day was over. In harvest season we had three. Our dress was of towcloth; for the children nothing but a shirt; for the older ones a pair of pantaloons or a gown in addition, according to the sex. Besides these, in the winter a round jacket or overcoat, a wool hat once in two or three years, for the males, and a pair of coarse shoes once a year.

We lodged in log huts, and on the bare ground. Wooden floors were an unknown luxury. In a single room were huddled, like cattle, ten or a dozen persons, men, women and children. All ideas of refinement and decency were, of course, out of the question. There were neither bedsteads, nor furniture of any description. Our beds were collections of straw and old rags, thrown down in the corners and boxed in with boards; a single blanket the only covering. Our favorite way of sleeping, however, was on a plank, our heads raised on an old jacket and our feet toasting before the smoldering fire. The wind whistled and the rain and snow blew in through the cracks, and the damp earth soaked in the moisture till the floor was miry as a pig-sty. Such were our houses. In these wretched hovels were we penned at night, and fed by day; here were the children born and the sick — neglected.

Josiah Henson, who wrote of field-hand life, was a slave until 1830, when he escaped to Canada.

Josiah Henson,
Truth Stranger than Fiction, 1858.

PRIMARY SOURCE *Guaranteed*

We Change — Traditions Remain

Traditions, whether music for the ear, food for the body, or stories for the soul, are called folkways. Folkways are important expressions of every culture and nation. Folkways keep heritage and history alive. They are bridges from one generation to the next. For immigrants, folkways are bridges to their homeland; links to the memories, people, and traditions of the past. Folkways carry on the traditions of a people from one generation to the next.

Africans who were taken by force into slavery came from many diverse, rich cultures in their homelands. Traditions of music, dance, crafts, and storytelling were as different from each other as their tribal ancestries.

Since Africans did not choose to come to the United States and the Caribbean islands, they could not bring treasured heirlooms, musical instruments, or tools necessary for crafts or artwork the way other immigrants did. The African love of music, dancing, and storytelling did continue in slavery-era black culture. However, the songs, movement, and stories changed as each new generation got further from its African roots.

Many African crafts, such as basket making, metallurgy, jewelry making, and weaving were not common in slavery. Other traditions, such as drumming, singing African songs, and dancing were outlawed by slave owners. Drumming was recognized as a way for slaves to send secret messages to each other. Therefore, it was forbidden. In addition, masters wanted their slaves to forget their African tongues. Use of native languages, even in songs, was punishable by beating. Indeed, slave traders took pains to separate slaves from the same tribe to prevent too many slaves with a common language from living in any one region of the Americas.

Slaves, however, did not forget their homeland, even after generations had passed their lives in bondage. They sang their sorrow in gospel songs with the rhythms and tunes of African songs. They continued stories common in their African homelands. Stories about Anansi the spider and Brer Rabbit, for example, have roots in African folklore. And, in the dark secrecy of night, slaves signaled from plantation to plantation with drumming — where drums were forbidden, slaves sometimes used hollow logs. Often, the stories and the drumming patterns did include secret messages — messages about how the slaves could triumph over their masters or find freedom.

The projects in the Folkways in a Nation of Immigrants segment of this unit will provide you with opportunities to learn about and experience the traditions of West Africa and traditions that survived the transition to slavery and beyond.

Folkways in a Nation of Immigrants

The following projects will help you learn about the traditions and folkways of immigrants from Africa. Learning and enjoying the art, food, stories, music, drama, and crafts of other cultures is like opening a window into the history and heritage of other people. You will experience traditions still practiced in Africa today. And you will learn to appreciate traditions practiced by your neighbors and fellow Americans.

❧ Adinkra cloth is a special kind of patterned cloth that is worn by some West African peoples, especially in Ghana. Each symbol or pattern on the cloth has a meaning that is special to the wearer. The patterns symbolize concepts, feelings, ideas, and objects. Your teacher has instructions and patterns for how to make your own Adinkra cloth. Show your cloth to the class and explain the meaning of the symbol or symbols you have created. **NOTE: This project involves sharp cutting tools and should be done under the supervision of a teacher or parent.**

❧ Your teacher has instructions for making a rock painting like the ones from ancient Africa. Create a painting based on an event in your life.

❧ Prepare the recipe for red beans and rice found at the end of this section. Or find and make another African American recipe. Bring your dish in to share with the class.

❧ Find recipes from one West African nation. Prepare a dish to share with your class. If the food is often served as part of a holiday or celebration, tell your class about the traditions associated with this food.

❧ Learn about West African crafts. Find out what traditional folk arts, such as basket weaving or mask making, are common to the region. Using pictures, drawings, or examples you make yourself, show your class one regional craft.

❧ Read the book *Be a Friend: The Story of African American Music in Song, Words, and Pictures,* by Leotha Stanley, to find out about African music, as well as spirituals and other kinds of music. Learn the song "Great Day" or another spiritual. You can find the words and music to "Great Day" in *Be A Friend*. Teach your class the words to the song you choose, and explain how slaves used these songs to send messages and express the words of freedom they were forbidden to say. Why were spirituals so important to the slaves?

❧ Find and learn a West African folktale. Tell it to your class.

❧ Find an Anansi (sometimes spelled Ananse) tale from Africa and one either from the United States or the Caribbean. Tell or read both to your class. Examine the differences between the two. Why do you think the stories changed?

❧ Find a story about Brer Rabbit or Brer Fox. Learn it and tell it to your class. Talk about the different purposes these stories had: to entertain, to express ideas their masters wouldn't let them say, to send messages, and so on. Explain the different meanings of the story you choose to your class. What is the lesson of your story? Now write your own story about these characters, in the same style.

Folkways in a Nation of Immigrants

❧ Jazz and blues are musical styles that were created by African Americans. Many experts consider them the only truly "American" forms of music. Find some tapes or CDs of blues or early jazz and play them for your class. What makes this music special? What do you think of it? Now, work on your own blues song.

❧ Go out at night and find the North Star. Follow it, checking your direction with a compass, to see what escaping slaves tried to do, making their way on the Underground Railroad.

❧ Have classmates pack you inside a sturdy box "addressed" to another class in your school, and have them "deliver" you to the class. After you are "opened," tell the class about Henry "Box" Brown, a slave who had himself shipped to the Anti-Slavery Society office in Philadelphia. Also, tell these students true stories about the escapes of other slaves. **IMPORTANT: Make sure your teacher approves this project and assists you with the packing and delivery!**

❧ Learn Ashanti (Asante) string games or other West African children's games. Teach one to your class.

❧ Learn about ceremonial masks from Ghana, Gambia, and the Ivory Coast. Find examples of some of these masks. Using papier mâché, create your own mask.

Folkways in a Nation of Immigrants

Red Beans and Rice

RED BEANS:

1. Soak beans overnight in 1 gallon cold water.

2. The next day, drain water from beans. Wash beans in cold water. Place beans in a medium stock pot.

3. Add one gallon cold water and salt. Cover and bring to a boil. Boil for 30 minutes.

4. Dice onion and green pepper.

5. Add onion, green pepper, black pepper, and garlic powder to beans.

6. Reduce heat to simmer or low. Cook uncovered an additional 30 minutes, or until beans are soft.

RICE:

1. Wash rice in strainer.

2. Under high heat, boil rice with 2 cups water and ½ teaspoon of salt.

3. Cover and simmer for an additional 15 minutes.

4. Strain.

Optional:
Dice 1 pound smoked turkey breast and add it when you add vegetables.

INGREDIENTS

1 — 2-pound bag of red beans

1 — medium onion

½ green pepper

2 tablespoons salt

1 tablespoon black pepper

1 tablespoon garlic powder

2 cups uncooked rice

(OPTIONAL):
1 pound smoked turkey breast

Folkways in a Nation of Immigrants

Rock Painting

MATERIALS NEEDED:

acrylic water-based paints

clay or small rocks about the size of baseballs

a watercolor brush

waterproof felt-tipped pens

OPTIONAL:

A jar of gesso, available at crafts stores. This material will smooth out minor imperfections on rock and clay and give you a better surface to draw on.

Ancient Africans told about their life by painting on rocks, walls, cliffs, or in caves. Rock paintings were used to show changes in the community and to mark special occasions such as hunts or moving from one place to another.

Now you can make your own rock painting with the materials here. Find a small rock or form one out of clay. After the clay dries, paint a story about something that happened in your community using the paint and felt-tipped pens. Usually you can only show the most important part of an event on a single painting. You might also try drawing a complete story on a large piece of paper.

On a separate sheet of paper, write a story about the painting you made.

Folkways in a Nation of Immigrants

NOTE:
Because sharp cutting tools are necessary, this project should be done under the supervision of a teacher, parent, or other adult.

MATERIALS NEEDED:

drawing paper

a linoleum tile, potato cut in half, or artgum eraser for making a stamp.

a sharp knife or safety razor

a black ink pad

cloth to print on, such as an old sheet or pillowcase

an old drop cloth, to help set design

distilled white vinegar

comb

good luck

Adinkra cloth

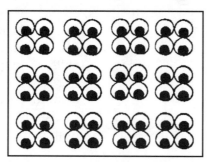

Adinkra cloth is a special type of cloth made by some peoples in Ghana, West Africa. A single geometric pattern or symbol is printed over and over in rows over one section of the cloth. (See examples.) An entire cloth may contain one or several symbols. The symbols stand for feelings, ideas, and objects.

Below are some traditional Adinkra cloth symbols, with their meanings. Try to come up with stories or explanations for how these patterns came to symbolize what they do.

Now, design a symbol and make your own Adinkra cloth.

INSTRUCTIONS:

1. Design a pattern or symbol for your cloth on a piece of paper. You can base your symbol on the traditional designs, or you can make up something entirely new. The symbol you settle on should have important meaning for you.

2. You will need to create a stamp with your design on it. To do this, trace your pattern onto a linoleum tile, potato, or artgum eraser with a pencil.

3. Using a knife or razor, cut out the background around your design on your stamp. You will want to follow your pencil tracing and cut the background away, so your design is raised up about a half an inch.

4. Press your stamp into the black ink pad and cover it well with ink. Then press your stamp onto the piece of cloth. Repeat.

5. Stamp your design in rows over the whole piece of cloth. (See examples above.)

6. To set the stamp design and keep it from running, soak an old cloth in distilled white vinegar. Place the cloth over your Adinkra cloth print and iron it until it is completely dry.

hair

agreement

first Adinkra symbol

knowledge

Research & Writing Topics

The following list includes suggestions for individual or group research and writing projects for this unit on immigrants from West Africa.

- ❧ Choose a fiction book about immigrants from Africa or about African Americans who moved North and West after slavery to establish new lives as homesteaders, farmers, and tradespeople. Write a book report telling the class about the story and its meaning to you. Note: this movement is different from the "Great Migration" that took place in the early 20th century.

- ❧ Trace a large map of West Africa. Using magazines, photocopied pictures from library and reference books, and on-line graphics, find pictures of as many cultural or ethnic groups in this region as possible. Look especially for illustrations of dress, traditions, or cultural lifestyles. Attach pictures to show where people live. Write captions under your photos giving information about each ethnic group, its people, traditions, and unique ways.

- ❧ Most slaves came from West Africa. Research the history of this area to find out where and from what tribes these captives came. Find out how they were kidnapped and brought to the Americas. Write a report on what you learn. Trace a map and note the homelands of these slaves.

- ❧ What is the Middle Passage? The "Rum Route"? How did slave traders make their fortunes? Find out about how traders treated their human cargo aboard slave ships. What happened? Write a report on what you learn.

- ❧ Kidnapped Africans did not easily submit to slavery. Find out about the following:
    the Amistad Mutiny, Cinque, Toussaint L'Ouverture
  Write a report about these people and events.

- ❧ Research what daily life was like for children and adults in slavery. Find out how people lived, ate, dressed, and worked. Find out how slave owners controlled and limited the lives of their slaves to avoid rebellion. Write a report about what you learn.

- ❧ Who were the Maroons? Find out about the experience of escaped slaves and Native American tribes. How did the U.S. government react to escaped slaves living with Native American tribes? What did the tribes do? Were there any that kept slaves themselves? Write a report about this little-known part of African American history.

- ❧ Find out how cotton is grown, picked, and processed. Why was the cotton gin so important to the southern economy, and how did its invention give a new boost to slavery? Why did "King Cotton" make the South so dependent upon slave labor? How did this affect the history of slavery? Write a report about what you learn.

- ❧ Choose two of the following to research and write about:
    Henry "Box" Brown, William and Ellen Craft, William Still, Nat Turner, Robert Smalls, Gabriel Prosser, Denmark Vesey

Research & Writing Topics

West Africa

❧ The role of abolitionists and the Underground Railroad was important in black history. Although many slaves freed themselves by escape and flight, the help of whites and free blacks sometimes made the difference between freedom and capture. Learn about the history of the Underground Railroad. Here are some topics, names, and words to help you:

Thomas Garrett, Levi Coffin, Lucretia Mott, Harriet Tubman, Frederick Douglass — *North Star*, Thomas Wentworth Higginson, Harriet Beecher Stowe — *Uncle Tom's Cabin*, William Lloyd Garrison — the *Liberator*, American Anti-Slavery Society, pattyrollers, David Walker — *Freedman's Journal*, John Brown, Fugitive Slave Law, Philadelphia Vigilance Committee

❧ Find out about anti-slavery groups, abolitionists, or events in the history of the region where you live that may have contributed to the end of slavery. For example, midwestern students may wish to research the history of the Detroit anti-slavery group called African American Mysteries: The Order of the Men of Oppression, or Wisconsin's Milton House Inn. In Massachusetts, students may find out about the League of Gileadites. State historical societies are good sources for this type of information. Write a report about what you learn.

❧ Learn about these laws and court rulings:
Fugitive Slave Law, Dred Scott Case, Compromise of 1850.
Find out what happened and why they were important, and write a report about what you learn.

❧ Write a report on either Harriet Tubman or Frederick Douglass. Find out as much as you can about their lives in slavery, their escapes, and their lives during and after the Civil War. How did each contribute to the struggle for freedom?

❧ Find out what happened to freed slaves after the Civil War. Here are some terms and topics to help:
Bureau of Refugees, Freedmen, and Abandoned Lands, or Freedmen's Bureau; black codes; Ku Klux Klan; Homestead Act; Civil Rights Act of 1866; carpetbaggers; "separate but equal" doctrine

❧ In some states, escaped slaves and, later, freedmen established African American communities. Nicodemus, Kansas; Yankton, South Dakota; and Pleasant Ridge, Wisconsin are just three of many such settlements. Find out if any towns or communities began in your state as settlements of escaped slaves and/or freedmen. Write a report on the founding, growth, and history of such communities. Your state's historical society is a good place to start research.

❧ The Homestead Act opened western territories for settlement. Some freedmen and former slaves became homesteaders. Find out about the history of black homesteaders. Write a report about what you learn. The state historical societies of Kansas, Missouri, Oklahoma, North Dakota, South Dakota, Montana, and Wyoming may be good sources of information.

Research & Writing Topics

West Africa

🐦 Research the history of Liberia, a country that began as a homeland for freed black slaves. How did the country begin? What has its history been? Did freed slaves relocate there? Place Liberia on a map of Africa. Write a report about what you learn.

🐦 In many places it was against the law for slaves to learn to read and write. Yet some slaves did learn — often in secret — and they wrote the stories of their own lives down in books called "slave narratives." Read a slave narrative. Write a book report describing what the book was about and what you thought about it. What was this slave's life like? What happened to him? Why do you think slave owners thought it was so important to keep slaves from learning to read and write?

🐦 Write a report about Ned, the slave who invented a cotton scraper, which his master tried to take the credit for.

🐦 The artist Jacob Lawrence collected a series of paintings he did called *The Migration Series* in a book. Find the book and report on it. What is the book about? Did you like the art? Why or why not? All the paintings have captions. Together, the paintings tell a story. Retell the story of the paintings in your own words.

🐦 The book *Sweet Words So Brave: The Story of African American Literature,* by Barbara K. Curry and James Michael Brodie, gives an overview of how African American literature developed from slave days up to the present. The book is divided into five time periods. Pick a time that is interesting to you. Research the authors and poets who were writing during the time period you choose. Write an essay about how their works fit into the time; that is, how they related to how African Americans were living.

🐦 The Harlem Renaissance was a time when many African American writers became prominent. Perhaps the most famous of them was Langston Hughes. Find a book of stories or poems written by Mr. Hughes and do a book report on it. What did you think of his work? What was he trying to say in his writing?

🐦 The Great Migration saw millions of African Americans moving from the rural South to the urban North, and finally throughout all of the United States. Do research on why families moved. Where did they move to? What culture did they bring with them, and what did they leave behind? What were their lives like in their new homes? Were they better or worse than the lives they'd left behind? Why?

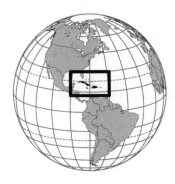

The Caribbean Islands

NOTE TO TEACHERS:
The materials on the student pages that follow are intended to provide your students with background, project ideas, and topics for research. You may choose to share some or all of these pages directly with your students. Or you may choose to adapt and format them to fit your own schedule, curriculum, and philosophy.

This unit on immigrants from the Caribbean islands will focus on the nations of Haiti, Cuba, and the Dominican Republic. Citizens of Puerto Rico, a Commonwealth of the United States, also hold citizenship in the United States. Although they are not technically immigrants, this unit will also include information on them. Although there are other nations, including the Cayman Islands and Bermuda, in the Caribbean islands, few immigrants from these countries have settled in the United States.

The Caribbean islands had slaves, but in many cases, the slaves revolted and freed themselves. Students will be encouraged to think about how more than 300 years of slavery, with their attendant evils of illiteracy, broken family structure, loss of power, suppression of language and culture, and lack of self-government, have made a lasting impact on the kinds of governments and cultures that exist today.

Students will be encouraged also to consider how new factors such as economic opportunity and political freedom factor in the decision to emigrate. Unique situations, such as the existence of Little Havana in Miami, Florida, or the large Puerto Rican settlements in New York City make for interesting research projects as well.

Once again, students will be asked to think about why people immigrate, and how their motivation for resettlement affects how well and where they settle in America.

The following ideas would enhance and further develop this unit:

❧ Invite a community member from an island nation to speak to the class about his or her own experience as an immigrant.

❧ Contact local VFW organizations to find a veteran who may have served with U.S. forces in the Caribbean. Ask this person to speak to your class about his or her experience.

❧ A staff member at a local university music department or community cultural center may know someone who plays steel drums. Ask this person to demonstrate this unique instrument to your class and tell how these drums are made and played.

❧ The music department of a local university may include scholars who have studied the history of African music and its influence on the musical styles of the Caribbean. If such a scholar lives in your area, ask him or her to speak to your class.

❧ Obtain tapes of music by groups like Sweet Honey in the Rock (Jazz, African-inspired Gospel), Bob Marley (reggae), and other island-based music.

❧ Ask if any students of Caribbean background have relatives who immigrated to the U.S. Invite them to tell the class about their experience as immigrants.

❧ Set aside a single time for students to share food, crafts, and projects from the We Change — Traditions Remain and Folkways in a Nation of Immigrants portions of this unit.

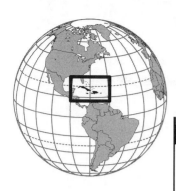

Why They Came to America

The following is a brief history of the people who came to the United States from the Caribbean area — Cuba, Haiti, the Dominican Republic, and Puerto Rico.

CUBA The vast majority of Cuban immigrants have come to the United States after 1959. In that time, well over one million Cubans have emigrated from their island nation, 90 miles from Florida. Most if not all of these people came here as refugees from Fidel Castro's communist government. It has been the policy of the United States to give shelter to all Cubans seeking entry into this country. However, in 1995, this policy underwent some changes, and the U.S. now wants to limit the number of Cubans that come here.

In 1959, Mr. Castro overthrew the regime of Fulgencio Batista. The first Cuban refugees were the allies of Mr. Batista, many of them business executives, industry leaders, and people with close ties to the United States. These people believed that their time in the U.S. would be short. They were confident that Mr. Castro would be thrown out of office himself. But a 1961 invasion of Cuba called the Bay of Pigs failed, and led to the emigration of another 150,000 Cubans. Many of these immigrants were doctors, lawyers, teachers, skilled workers, and businesspeople. People emigrated steadily until after the Cuban Missile Crisis in 1962, when the U.S. and the Soviet Union almost went to war over the installation of Soviet nuclear missiles in Cuba. After the Soviet Union withdrew its missiles, Mr. Castro closed all air traffic between Cuba and the U.S. From 1962 to the 1970s, Cuban immigrants left the island in boats or rafts. The situation changed in the 1970s, when Mr. Castro authorized "Freedom Flights" in airplanes for those who wished to leave the country. It changed again in 1980, when Mr. Castro allowed more than 100,000 Cubans to leave in what was called the "Mariel Boatlift." In the 1980s and 1990s, the exodus continues, as many Cubans flee to the U.S. in boats and rafts, or with the help of relatives already here.

HAITI Haiti and the Dominican Republic share an island called Hispaniola. Haiti is the poorest country in the Western Hemisphere. Christopher Columbus explored Hispaniola in 1492, and claimed it for Spain. Shortly after Spanish colonists reached the island, they moved to where the Dominican Republic now is, and the other half of the island — Haiti — was claimed by France. Both countries imported slaves from West Africa to farm sugar cane and coffee, because almost all of the enslaved natives on the island died. In 1791, the slaves revolted. Their leader, Toussaint L'Ouverture, took over the entire island. France and Spain regained control of their colonies in 1801, but another revolt expelled them in 1822. Both Haiti and the Dominican Republic set up their own governments.

From the 1950s through the early 1990s, Haiti was ruled by cruel dictators who gathered much of the existing wealth for themselves. In the 1970s and 1980s, many Haitian people tried to escape the repressive political system and terrible poverty of their nation. They left their nation for other Caribbean, Central American, and South American nations, and for the U.S. The first Haitian immigrants here were professionals — mostly working in medicine and the law. But for many years now, poor people have attempted to leave the country, along with those in danger from the government.

Why They Came to America

In 1990, a repressive regime was overthrown and Jean-Bertrand Aristide, a former Catholic priest, was chosen president of Haiti in the country's first free election. But eight months after Mr. Aristide took office, he was ousted by some members of the military. From that point in 1991 until 1994, when he was returned to office through efforts of the United States, thousands of Haitians tried to escape their country. Most of them left in rickety boats, and many died trying to reach other lands. Many were rescued by the U.S. Coast Guard and taken to the Guantanamo Naval Base in Cuba. When Mr. Aristide was returned to power, the flight of the boat people stopped, but many Haitians who had already fled did not want to return to their country. About 15,000 Haitians were kept at the base, waiting either for their return to Haiti, or their admission to the U.S.

DOMINICAN REPUBLIC Like Haiti, the Dominican Republic's history is spotted with oppression and dictators. The early years saw the Dominican Republic side of Hispaniola colonized by the Spanish. After Hispaniola gained its independence in 1822, dictators and military strongmen ruled both sides of the island. In 1965, dictator Rafael Trujillo was assassinated. U.S. Marines went to the island to restore order. Since 1965, thousands of immigrants from the Dominican Republic have moved to the United States. Most of them come here to escape the poverty that dominates the entire island of Hispaniola.

The Dominicans who first came to this country were professionals looking to advance their careers. Later immigrants were poorer. Many of the immigrants settled in large urban centers. Today, there are large settlements of recent immigrants from the Dominican Republic in New York City and Chicago.

PUERTO RICO Strictly speaking, Puerto Ricans who come to the United States are not immigrants. They are citizens of the United States. In 1898, the U.S. took possession of Puerto Rico from Spain following the Spanish-American War. In 1917, Puerto Rico was granted a special "Commonwealth" status that provided U.S. citizenship to all residents of the island.

By 1930, more than 50,000 Puerto Ricans had moved to the mainland, most of them settling in New York City. After World War Two ended in 1945, migration to the U.S. boomed. Puerto Rico had problems with overpopulation, under-employment, and poverty. Improvement in air travel and inexpensive one-way tickets to the mainland helped bring about the first airborne migration in history of people from one land to another. By 1955, an estimated 675,000 Puerto Ricans were living on the mainland, with an estimated 500,000 living in New York City. By 1980, two million people of Puerto Rican descent were living on the U.S. mainland. Today, there are an estimated 2.7 million Puerto Ricans living here. Puerto Ricans have faced racism and unemployment here. And until recently, they have not been politically powerful because they haven't been organized. Many of the Puerto Ricans who moved here after World War Two dreamed of going back to their homeland after they earned enough money. Today, many Puerto Ricans feel that the mainland U.S. is their home.

In Their Own Words

NOTE TO TEACHERS:

The following documents relate the stories of children of immigrants living in New York City. One is by the author Piri Thomas, from his autobiography *Down These Mean Streets*, about his experiences as a Puerto Rican growing up in an Italian neighborhood. The other is a contemporary account by a 12-year-old girl whose parents came from the Dominican Republic.

The passage called "Alien Turf" relates an incident that happened in the 1940s. "A Dominican American in New York" was written by a 12-year-old in the 1990s. What similarities and differences can you see in the two accounts? What role do you think parents play in helping their children? Do you think prejudice against different groups has changed since the 1940s?

In Their Own Words

Alien Turf

In his 1967 autobiography *Down These Mean Streets*, author Piri Thomas recalls his struggles as a young Puerto Rican trying to fit into an Italian neighborhood in New York City during the 1940s.

Sometimes you don't fit in. Like if you're a Puerto Rican on an Italian block. After my new baby brother, Ricardo, died of some kind of germs, Poppa moved us from 111th Street to Italian turf on 114th Street between Second and Third Avenue. I guess Poppa wanted to get Momma away from the hard memories of the old pad.

I sure missed 111th Street, where everybody acted, walked, and talked like me. But on 114th Street everything went all right for a while. There were a few dirty looks from the spaghetti-an'-sauce cats, but no big sweat. Till that one day I was on my way home from school and almost had reached my stoop when someone called: "Hey, you dirty … spic."

The words hit my ears and almost made me curse Poppa at the same time. I turned around real slow and found my face pushing in the finger of an Italian kid about my age. He had five or six of his friends with him.

"Hey you," he said. "What nationality are ya?"…

My voice was almost shy in its anger. "I'm Puerto Rican," I said. "I was born here." I wanted to shout it, but it came out like a whisper.

"Right here inna street?" Rocky sneered. "Ya mean right here inna middle of da street?"

They all laughed.

I hated them. I shook my head slowly from side to side. "Uh-uh," I said softly. "I was born inna hospital — inna bed."

"Ummm, paisan — born inna bed," Rocky said.

I didn't like Rocky Italiano's voice. "Inna hospital," I whispered, and all the time my eyes were trying to cut down the long distance from this trouble to my stoop. But it was no good; I was hemmed in by Rocky's friends. I couldn't help thinking about kids getting wasted for moving into a block belonging to other people.

"What hospital, paisan?" Bad Rocky pushed.

"Harlem Hospital," I answered, wishing like all hell that it was 5 o'clock instead of just 3 o'clock, 'cause Poppa came home at 5. I looked around for some friendly faces belonging to grown-up people, but the elders were all busy yakking away in Italian. I couldn't help thinking how much like Spanish it sounded. …

"Ain't that right, kid?" Rocky pressed. "Ain't that where all black people get born?"

In Their Own Words

I dug some of Rocky's boys grinding and pushing and punching closed fists against open hands. I figured they were looking to shake me up, so I straightened up my humble voice and made like proud. "There's all kinds of people born there. Colored people, Puerto Ricans like me, an' — even spaghetti-benders like you."

"That's a dirty ... lie" — bash, I felt Rocky's fist smack into my mouth — "you dirty ... spic."

I got dizzy and ten more dizzy when fists started to fly from everywhere and only toward me. I swung back, splat, bish — my fist hit some face and I wished I hadn't, 'cause then I started getting kicked.

I heard people yelling in Italian and English and I wondered if maybe it was 'cause I hadn't fought fair in having hit that one guy. But it wasn't. The voices were trying to help me.

"What'sa matta, you no-good kids, leeva da kid alone," a man said. I looked through a swelling eye and dug some Italians pushing their kids off me with slaps. ...

"You all right, kiddo?" asked the man.

"Where you live, boy?" said another one.

"Is the bambino hurt?" asked a woman.

I didn't look at any of them. I felt dizzy. I didn't want to open my mouth to talk, 'cause I was fighting to keep from puking up. I just hoped my face was cool-looking. I walked away from that group of strangers. I reached my stoop and started to climb the stairs. ...

Momma was cooking, and the smell of rice and beans was beating the smell of Parmesan cheese from the other apartments. I let myself into our new pad. I tried to walk fast past Momma so I could wash up, but she saw me.

"My God, Piri, what happened?" she cried.

"Just a little fight in school, Momma. You know how it is, Momma, I'm new in school, an'..." I made myself laugh. Then I made myself say, "But Moms, I whipped the living ... outta two guys, an' one was bigger'n me."

"Bendito, Piri, I raise this family in Christian way. Not to fight. Christ says to turn the other cheek."

"Sure, Momma." I smiled and went and showered, feeling sore at Poppa for bringing us into spaghetti country. I felt my face with easy fingers and thought about all the running back and from school that was in store for me.

Piri Thomas, *Down These Mean Streets*, (New York: Alfred A. Knopf, 1967.)

In Their Own Words

Heidi Alvarez, a young girl living in New York City, describes her life as an American-born Dominican. She also discusses her Dominican-born parents' immigration to the United States and their struggle to live in New York. This piece was written when she was 12 years old.

A Dominican American in New York

My name is Heidi Alvarez. I'm twelve years old. … My parents both were born in Dominican Republic but me and my brother and sister were born here in New York City. …

It's weird and strange at the same time being Dominican but American-born because I have to practice both cultures. I mean at home I talk Spanish with my parents and eat Spanish food and some rules my parents give me are almost based on the rules their parents gave them, like I have to be at home at a certain time. I have to do some things. In school I have to talk English, at lunch time I have to eat American food, and basically in school I learn American history. …

Some people when they immigrate from my parents' homeland to U.S.A., after they become adjust to the American life they forget to celebrate some of their holidays. Some examples are: the Three Kings Days, the Dominican Independence Day, or sometimes the Dominican father-mother days. I think is very important that we celebrate these days because it shows you're still a Dominican at heart even though you're living in another country. Not only that, but your children will show their own children value.

When I have my own children I will let them be independent and I will also celebrate Domincan-American holidays because I think it's important that you show and teach them history from both cultures. …

My parents choose to come and live here in the United States of America. They move here from the Dominican Republic. My mother (Adriana) was born in a small town called San Francisco de Macoris and my father in Tenares. My mother went to school in the capital, Santo Domingo, to the University of Autonoma and study medical technology. She finish and married my father in 1979.

My father came first to New York City and lived in his mother's house because she was the one that brought him and his other 11 brothers and sister then later the next year, 1980, my mother came to New York. They lived in my aunt's house in a small room.

At first it was very hard for my mother. She didn't knew how to speak English, she work in a factory. By then, my mother and my father had their own apartment. Two years later she had me (1983). My mother decided it was time she move forward and become something of herself, something she could say she's proud of. In the daytime she took care of me, and in the night when my father came home from work, she went to English school to learn English. She did this routine until she learned, then when I started

In Their Own Words

school, she went to school. She study at Hostos [Community] College and study education then she went and study at Hunter College. Later she study at Baruch College and earned her bachelor degree. Recently now she's studying at City College to earn her master's degree. My parents came here because they wanted a better future with more opportunity for them and for me, my sister, and my brother. ...

I feel more Dominican than American because I'm proud of what I'm and because I'm always around Spanish-speaking people. This is my point of view from a child being born American but being raised by Dominicans. My parents taught a lesson to push myself and study and get the right education so I could achieve and become higher and higher. One day when I walk down the aisle with my future friends graduate I could say I'm proud of being a Dominican and also being a doctor or a lawyer. I would gladly stand up in front of millions of crowd and say I'm proud of both of my heritage. ...

We Change — Traditions Remain

Traditions, whether music for the ear, food for the body, or stories for the soul, are called folkways. Folkways are important expressions of every culture and nation. Folkways keep heritage and history alive. They are bridges from one generation to the next. For immigrants, folkways are bridges to their homeland; links to the memories, people, and traditions of the past. Folkways carry on the traditions of a people from one generation to the next.

The culture and traditions of the Caribbean islands are a fascinating mixture of Native, French, Spanish, and African history and heritage. Slaves brought their languages, musical heritage, and storytelling traditions. French colonists in Hispaniola and Spanish landowners in Cuba and Jamaica brought stringed instruments, traditional dancing, literature, and art from Europe. All these elements have melted together in a distinctive culture.

The Caribbean has a unique history. Where else would such different cultures meet and blend together? The music, art, foods, drama, stories, and dance of the Caribbean island countries has also been influenced by the poverty of the people. When European slave owners were driven out or left, these countries struggled to establish governments, schools, and trade. Generations of slaves had not been free to express themselves through things like art or theatre. Native customs had often been stamped out by colonial governments. Sometimes, the only literature available was European.

Music, dance, and storytelling, however, are folkways available to even the poorest and least educated people. For that reason, perhaps, music and storytelling have been some of the main ways Caribbean island people have expressed themselves creatively. Festivals and religious holiday celebrations are also important in the Caribbean. In Cuba, where the communist government has outlawed religious holidays, political festivals have been substituted. And the Central American tradition of mural painting is also popular and beautiful. As you explore the folkways of the Caribbean, you will discover many of the interesting traditions of these multicultural people.

Folkways in a Nation of Immigrants

The following projects will help you learn about the traditions and folkways of Caribbean island immigrants. Learning and enjoying the art, food, stories, music, drama, and crafts of other cultures is like opening a window into the history and heritage of other people. You will experience traditions still practiced in the Caribbean islands today. And you will learn to appreciate traditions practiced by your neighbors and fellow Americans.

❧ Prepare the recipe for sweet potato pudding found in this section. Or prepare another dish from a Caribbean island culture. If the food is served most often during a holiday or celebration, tell your class about the traditions associated with this food.

❧ Learn how sugar is produced from cane. Buy sugar cane for your class to sample. Tell them what you learned.

❧ Find out about one of these famous Americans from the Caribbean. Tell your class about his or her life, accomplishments, and contributions to society:
Justino Diaz, José Feliciano, Roberto Clemente, Pablo Casals, José Canseco, Gloria Estefan, Julia Alvarez

❧ What are steel drums? How are they made? How are they used? Find out what you can. Also, find a record, tape, video, or CD of steel drum music to share with your class.

❧ Christmas is an important holiday on most Caribbean islands. Choose one country and learn about its Christmas traditions. Bring in either traditional decorations, music, or foods for the class to sample. Tell about what you learned.

❧ Learn about the history of one of these types of music common to the Caribbean: Salsa, Jazz, Reggae, and Mambo. What instruments are used? Where is the music commonly heard today? Where did it come from originally? Who are or were famous performers? Bring in a record, tape, or CD of this musical style. Tell the class what you learned.

❧ What does it mean to be a Creole? What is the Creole language? What is special about Creole food? Find out about this language and culture. Find out some Creole words to share with your class. Give a brief oral report about what you learn.

❧ Learn about Jamaican carnival masks. Make one to show to your class. Tell how they are made and used.

❧ Find out about Cuban mural art. Although much of this art is now done with government funding and uses political and social themes, it is still a unique art form. Find out how the countryside, large city, or seashore looks in Cuba. Design and paint a mural on large pieces of paper in the style of Cuban mural painting.

❧ Learn a folktale from one Caribbean island country. Tell it aloud to your class.

❧ Find folktales from more than one country in the Caribbean. Using island music as a background, tell one or two of these stories to a class of younger children.

Folkways in a Nation of Immigrants

🕷 Learn an Anansi the Spider story from the Caribbean and an Anansi story from Africa. Tell both to your class. How are they the same? How are they different?

Sweet Potato Pudding

INGREDIENTS

3 — medium sweet potatoes

1 cup grated coconut

2 tablespoons butter or margarine

1 tablespoon grated ginger

½ cup brown sugar

¼ teaspoon nutmeg

½ teaspoon cinnamon

2 teaspoons vanilla extract

1 cup milk

1. Peel, wash and grate potatoes. Add grated coconut and combine well

2. Add butter or margarine, ginger, sugar, nutmeg, cinnamon, and vanilla. Mix well.

3. Add milk and mix again.

4. Pour mixture into a greased baking dish. Bake at 350 degrees for about one hour, or until all the liquid is absorbed and the pudding is golden brown.

Serve

Research & Writing Topics

The following list includes suggestions for individual or group research and writing projects for this unit on immigrants from Caribbean Islands.

- ❦ Choose a fiction book about immigrants from the Caribbean islands in America or about life in the Caribbean. Write a book report telling the class about the story and its meaning to you.

- ❦ Trace a large map of the Caribbean. Using magazines, photocopied pictures from library and reference books, and on-line graphics, find pictures of as many cultural/ethnic groups in the Caribbean as possible. Look especially for illustrations of national costumes, traditions, or cultural lifestyles. Attach pictures to show where different groups of people live. Write captions under your photos giving information about the ethnic group, its people, traditions, and unique ways.

- ❦ Haiti has been called "Daughter of Africa" because much of its population is descended from African slaves. Find out who Toussaint L'Ouverture was. What did he do? Why was he important to Haiti and other Caribbean island people? Write a report about what you learn.

- ❦ From 1981 to 1990, 252,000 people from the Dominican Republic came to America as immigrants. Why did most of these people come to the United States? What were their lives like in their homeland? Where did they settle? What customs and traditions do these immigrants continue? Write a report about what you discover in your research.

- ❦ Learn about the history of Haiti and "Papa Doc" and "Baby Doc" Duvalier. What effect did their rule have on Haiti today? How do you think that has affected emigration? What kind of government does Haiti have now? How has Haiti's history shaped the government it has today? Write a report about what you learn.

- ❦ Who is Jean-Bertrand Aristide? What role did the United States play in his political life in Haiti? Write a report about what you learn.

- ❦ Puerto Rico has been called "The 51st State." Find out what kind of relationship exists between Puerto Rico and the United States. Do Puerto Ricans vote? Are they citizens? What kind of financial and economic ties exist? What kind of government does Puerto Rico have? School system? Economy? What is life like in Puerto Rico? Write a report about what you learn.

- ❦ Learn about the history of Cuba in the 20th century. Here are some topics and words to help you in your research:

  Fulgencio Batista; Fidel Castro; Che Guevara; 26 of July Movement; Bay of Pigs invasion; Guantanamo Naval Base; Mariel Exodus; "Freedom Flights"; Antonio Maceo Brigade; Little Havana — Miami, Florida.

  Learn about Cuban history. Think about how this history has affected Cuban immigration to the United States. Write a report about what you learn. This topic might work well as a group project.

Research & Writing Topics

The Caribbean Islands

❧ Do research about Cuban "boat people." Using magazines and newspapers, find out how, when, and why they came to the United States. What has the U.S. government done in response? What has the Cuban government done? Think about the differences between an immigrant and a refugee. What has U.S. policy been toward Cuban immigrants? Is that policy changing? Why do you think the U.S. government gives some people political asylum and not others? Write a report about what you learn.

❧ Many Caribbean nations were slave-populated colonies from 1510, when the French brought the first slaves to Hispaniola (the island that holds Haiti and the Dominican Republic) until the 1880s when slavery was finally stamped out in Cuba. Slave owners kept slaves illiterate. The island of Puerto Rico did not even have a printing press until the late 1860s. The French and Spanish governments denied even freed blacks the right to vote or become citizens. Slaves had no experience in self-government. Find out about the history of slavery on one of the Caribbean islands. Learn how the slaves were freed, what occurred then, and what kind of government the island has had since that time. Imagine how the centuries of slavery affected the ability of people to govern themselves when slavery ended. How do you think that has affected the recent history of the island? How do you think it has affected emigration from the island? Write a report about what you learn and tell what you think about these questions.

❧ Research the history of piracy in the Caribbean. Find out about links between piracy and the slave trade. Write a report about what you learn.

❧ The Caribbean was part of the Middle Passage during the era of slave trade. Find out about the transport of slaves from Africa to the Caribbean and to the United States. Research the "Rum Route" to find out how slave traders made money.

Mexico & Central America

NOTE TO TEACHERS:
The materials on the student pages that follow are intended to provide your students with background, project ideas, and topics for research. You may choose to share some or all of these pages directly with your students. Or you may choose to adapt and format them to fit your own schedule, curriculum, and philosophy. This unit also includes craft instructions that you can photocopy and distribute to your students.

This unit on Mexican and Central American immigrants will focus on the history, people, and cultures of Mexico, Nicaragua, El Salvador, and Guatemala.

Since the history of these nations, particularly the recent history of Nicaragua, El Salvador, and Guatemala, has been filled with violence, political oppression, and revolution, this study may raise some difficult questions and issues in the classroom. Students may wonder why the U.S. government funded and supported the Contras in Nicaragua. Students may wonder why the U.S. refused asylum to refugees fleeing civil war or revolution in these countries. Use of films like *Roses in December* or *Romero* may give rise to spirited or intense classroom discussion. Discussion of immigrants from Central America, like the history of these nations, is not about absolute good versus absolute bad. Teachers may be challenged to help students understand how and why the United States was allied with one side against another.

Immigrants from Mexico and other Central American countries have been in the news for the past three or four decades. Whether the issue is legal rights for migrant workers, sanctuary for refugees fleeing civil war in El Salvador, or public education for children of illegal immigrants, our southern neighbors have impacted our industry, schools, tax dollars, and public services. Students may be surprised to see the extent of that impact.

The following suggestions might enhance or further develop this unit. Teachers should consider whether they are possible or appropriate for their classes.

- Contact area high schools to see if any exchange students from Mexico or other Central American countries would like to share with your class information about their homelands.

- Check library or inter-library loan resources for tapes or CDs of Latin music.

- Contact area university art departments to determine if there are any local textile weavers familiar with backstrap looms and Guatemalan weaving.

- Contact area churches, refugee settlement support organizations, or church denominational leaders to find out whether any local people were involved in the "sanctuary movement." Invite someone to speak to your class about this experience.

- If Chicano or Latino families have settled in your community, invite an adult or young person to share his or her experience coming to the United States from Mexico or Central America.

☙ Ask if any students of Mexican or Central American background have relatives who immigrated to the U.S. Invite them to tell the class about their experience as immigrants.

☙ Set aside a single time for students to share food, crafts, and projects from the We Change — Traditions Remain and Folkways in a Nation of Immigrants portions of this unit.

Why They Came to America

The following is a brief history of the people who came to the United States from Mexico, Nicaragua, El Salvador, and Guatemala.

MEXICO More immigrants come to the United States from Mexico than from any other single country. Census estimates say there are more than 13 million people of Mexican descent living in the United States. These 13 million are the biggest share of America's fastest growing ethnic group — Latinos. Latinos are people whose families came originally from a Latin American nation. There are an estimated 27 million Latinos living in the U.S. — a little more than 10 percent of the total population.

The majority of Mexican immigrants have come here for two main reasons. The first is to leave behind unstable or dangerous political situations in their home country. The second is to escape poverty and find work in this country.

The first Mexicans to live within the boundaries of the United States were not immigrants at all. They were members of Spanish-descended families living in territories taken from Mexico after a war in the 1840s. The present states of Texas, California, Nevada, Utah, and parts of Arizona, New Mexico, and Colorado, once all belonged to Mexico. Many parts of this arid region were settled by Mexicans. Anglo Americans copied many Mexican ways of living on this dry land. For example, the Southwest's "ranch culture" — maintaining large tracts of land to raise livestock and tending the land with ranch hands and cowboys — came directly from the Mexican system. Anglo Americans also copied Mexican farming techniques.

U.S. authorities have long had an indecisive attitude toward actual Mexican immigrants. On the one hand, for decades the U.S. encouraged Mexicans to become migrant workers, so they could help farm and perform other tasks. Migrant workers move from place to place, harvesting crops as they ripen. On the other hand, the U.S. has tried to discourage the actual settlement of these workers here. All through the last part of the 19th and the early part of the 20th century, poor Mexicans were recruited to work in mines, on farms, and on railroads in the Southwest. It was understood that these workers would eventually go back to Mexico, although there was no law stopping them from taking up permanent residence in the United States. Many of them did. Before 1924, Mexicans and Americans freely crossed the border separating the two countries. In 1924, a U.S. border patrol was established, but with only 75 guards for 2,000 miles, it was ineffective.

In 1930, there were one million Mexicans living here. Most of them held migrant or other low-paying jobs. By 1940, that number had dropped to less than 400,000 because of hard economic times in this country and around the world. By 1942, with the U.S. involved in World War Two, a *bracero*, or "hired hand," program encouraged Mexican workers to come back here again. The program was put into place to fix a labor shortage that grew in the U.S. as millions of men were drafted into the military. The *bracero* program continued until 1965, and in that time millions of Mexican migrant workers entered

Why They Came to America

the country to follow the crop harvests, and then left again. But many other migrants established homes in the United States. Some found work in factories. Others got service jobs, like housecleaning, restaurant work, maintenance work, and other low- or semi-skilled jobs. Still others started their own businesses. Many people of Mexican descent live in large cities throughout the country. However, most Mexican Americans live in California, Texas, the other Southwestern states, and Illinois.

Mexicans and other Latinos are the objects of the latest debates about immigration in this country. Right now, about 800,000 immigrants are allowed to legally enter the U.S. each year. It is estimated that another 400,000 enter illegally, and most of these illegal immigrants are Latino. Lawmakers and others in California have often called for strengthening the border patrol system between Mexico and the U.S. In 1994, voters in California passed a referendum called Proposition 187, which called for cutting off social and medical services to illegal immigrants and their children. At the same time, Mexican and other Latino immigrants fill an important role in California's economy, as they do in Texas and other Southwestern states. Most experts think the question of immigration from Mexico to the U.S. will continue to spark political debate into the next century.

GUATEMALA, NICARAGUA, EL SALVADOR Significant immigration from these three countries began in the 1970s and continued through the 1980s. Most immigrants from these countries came here because of bitter political strife in their home countries. The exact number of Guatemalan, Nicaraguan, and Salvadoran immigrants to this country is unknown, because many of them came without documentation or as refugees. Many of these refugees hid their identities to avoid being sent back to their countries. Estimates say that from 500,000 to two million people came to the U.S. from these three countries. As the political situations in their countries have stabilized, many of them have returned home, although a significant number remain in the U.S.

In 1979, the unrest that had been brewing for a long time reached a climax in Nicaragua. The Sandinista rebel group forced Anastasio Somoza Debayle, the harsh leader of Nicaragua, into exile and took over the country. The United States opposed the revolution, saying that the Sandinistas were communists. The U.S. supported the "Contras." The Contras were anti-communists and members of Mr. Somoza's National Guard. They began attacking Nicaragua from the neighboring country of Honduras. The Sandinistas had been supported by most of the people of Nicaragua in their fight against Mr. Somoza. But their program of social reform was not fully accepted. Soon, a large portion of the Nicaraguan people supported the Contras. From 1980 to 1988, Nicaragua was in the grip of a civil war. Many thousands of people were killed on both sides. To escape the war, hundreds of thousands more left the country — many of them for the United States. A number of these refugees settled in cities in the southern and northeastern U.S.

Why They Came to America

Slightly larger than Massachusetts, El Salvador is the smallest country in Central America, but it also has the densest population of any mainland country in the Western Hemisphere. That means more people live on each square mile in El Salvador than in any other place in this half of the world. In the 1970s and '80s, the country was caught in a bitter civil war. In El Salvador at this time, a few wealthy families owned most of the land. The war was fought over redistributing much of this land to more of the people. In the war, small groups of rebels fought the army. Death squads that supported the government killed thousands of people. These death squads were groups that took the law into their own hands and killed people who opposed them. It is estimated that a quarter of El Salvador's population of five million left the country during the war. About 600,000 of them fled to the United States where many were given "sanctuary" by religious and other groups.

Guatemala, which lies just south of Mexico, is the third Central American country that has long had civil strife. In 1954, Guatemala's president was overthrown with the help of the U.S. Central Intelligence Agency, or CIA. The president was overthrown because some feared he was a communist sympathizer. From the early 1960s until the mid-1990's, a little-publicized civil war took place in Guatemala. The war was between the government, which was controlled by the military, and leftist, or communist, groups. Many human rights violations occurred, and many people in the rural areas of the country were killed. An estimated 130,000 people were killed in the 30 years of the fighting. All during this time, people fled Guatemala for other countries. Many settled in Mexico. Others came to the United States, again as part of the sanctuary movement started by some religious groups. At the end of 1996, there was real hope for peace as an agreement between military and rebel forces went into effect.

In Their Own Words

NOTE TO TEACHERS:

In this section, immigrants from Mexico and Guatemala tell why they came to America and how they adjusted to living here.

After reading these accounts, you might discuss with the class some of the following:

The first document is a letter a Mexican immigrant named Angela Gomez wrote to a friend. In one paragraph, she praises Fresno, California, for being clean and having nice parks. In the next paragraph, she talks about how dangerous it is. Why do you think the new immigrant finds her experience in Fresno to be mixed? Do you think she fears crime or the Border Patrol more? What difficulties do you think she faces because she doesn't speak English as well as she'd like to? How hard or easy would it be to move to another country and learn a new language?

The second story is the account of a woman named Elena Ixcot and her family who fled Guatemala. After reading her story, how important do you think education is in helping poor people lead better lives? Compare her story with Angela's. What difficulties do you think Elena faces in her new country? When this story was written, Elena and her family were part of the sanctuary movement. What do you think sanctuary means? Do you think it was right or wrong for groups to give sanctuary to people, often in defiance of U.S. laws?

In Their Own Words

Letter from a recent Mexican immigrant to her friend in the state of Jalisco, Mexico, translated from Spanish.

[from] Angela Gomez
Fresno, CA
March 5, 1988

[to] Mariana Garcia Chavez
Zapopan, Jalisco, Mexico

Hello Mariana!

Receive this letter, wishing that it finds you very well. A little late, you know I'm a little lazy about writing, but here it is, one of the first letters I write.

Right now I'm studying English, it's a little hard to find work, but at least I'm not wasting time. I go to a school for adults where it's just about pure Chinese, Japanese and Iranians, almost pure Asian, in one of the groups I go to I'm the only Mexican woman, two other Mexicans go besides me, and like some 50 Chinese. ... I'm learning quickly, I go every day and I take six hours a day. Aside from this I go to another school 3 days a week for just 2 hours a day. In this other school I have a black teacher who is really good people. So in a little while I'm going to be more or less speaking English, in the long run it's going to be useful to me somehow. Fresno, it's beautiful, it's a big city and has very few inhabitants, it's a very clean city, it has very beautiful parks (I was thinking of just writing a little ...)

At the moment it's really boring here because it gets dark really early, and it's really dangerous to wander the streets, there are tons of crazies, a mountain of robberies, murders, rapes, and everything you can imagine, it's a really hostile environment, and more so for Latinos.

About 22 days ago, in a city near here called Madera, an agent from the border patrol killed a 17-year-old boy, the agent came around asking for his papers, so the boy tried to run away, but the border patrol agent (almost two meters [about 6 feet] tall) grabbed him by the shirt and smashed him to the ground (the boy, Mexican, was very short and thin); the agent, even seeing the boy was bleeding, wasn't so good as to call an ambulance, but took him to jail instead, until later when they could see he was really hurt they took him to the hospital, but it was already too late, because a few hours later he died.

You hear about a mountain of abuses by the border patrol against Latinos all the time. ...

I love you,
Angelita

In Larry Siems, *Between the Lines: Letters Between Undocumented Mexican and Central American Immigrants and Their Families and Friends* (Hopewell, N.J.: The Ecco Press, 1992).

In Their Own Words

PRIMARY Guaranteed SOURCE

This is the story of Elena Ixcot, a Guatemalan, as told to the writer Sara Nelson.

"We Fled for Our Lives"

The day I arrived in the United States was both the happiest and the saddest day of my life. I was joyful because my family and I had managed to survive the dangerous 4,000-mile journey from our native Guatemala, but I was full of sorrow for my relatives and friends who remained there and for what had happened to my beloved country.

Until four years ago, Felipe and I were *campesinos* [farmers] in a small mountain village in Guatemala. We were typical villagers in most respects. We worked in the fields for large farming companies. We were very poor. We lived with our four children in a one-room hut and slept on straw mats. But were also very different from many other *campesinos*. While most of our neighbors speak only our Mayan dialect, both Felipe and I speak Spanish as well. And we both are educated — Felipe completed the fourth grade and I completed the third grade. ...

It turned out that education was our crime. Felipe and my younger brother, José, had begun to teach other *campesinos* how to read and write and how to join together to buy fertilizer and farm equipment. I was teaching the village women about nutrition. We were trying to improve ourselves and our lives. We wanted to be able to buy meat and milk for our children.

The government, however, thought that our activities were "subversive." One day, while Felipe was working in the fields and the older children and I were outside playing, someone set fire to our hut. Juanita, then two, was still inside. I ran through the flames and smoke to save her. She was sobbing, terrified. ...

Although Felipe and I had never once been separated in ten years of marriage, we both knew that he had to go away. Promising to send for the children and me as soon as he could, Felipe set off on foot for Guatemala City. For almost three years he lived there, using a different name and living on a plantation.

Meanwhile, I was trying to give my children as normal a life as possible. Because it was too dangerous for Felipe to return home, I thought it would be better to tell them that their father was dead. At any moment, I knew, my lie could have become truth, and I didn't want to give them any false hopes. ...

One day my brother José was called in for questioning. We didn't hear from him for three days. Then one morning a group of soldiers no older than he arrived at our door. "Did you know this man?" one of them asked, tossing the mutilated body of José onto the ground. I nodded, horrified, and then I began to cry.

The young soldier said, "I'm sorry, we discovered his body this morning. We think he was killed by leftists." Even in my grief I knew the soldier was

In Their Own Words

lying — José had angered no one but the government. The soldiers thought he was a "communist," so they killed him.

A little later, we learned from a Catholic priest that Felipe had left Guatemala City and had crossed the border into Chiapas, Mexico, to work on a coffee plantation. ... Just before dawn one morning in 1982, the children and I packed one bag and set out for Chiapas. ... [After four days] we arrived in Chiapas, tired, hungry, and with blistered feet. ... That night, there was a knock on the door of the hut where I was staying. I opened it and saw Felipe. He looked older and more tired than he ever had looked before, but there he was, smiling at me as if I'd never been away. It was like seeing a ghost. I was in shock — laughing, crying, and hugging him all at the same time. But as he came inside the hut Juanita, who was then four, began to scream: "Who is that man?" Felipe had been away from us so long that his daughter didn't remember her own father.

We all stayed in Chiapas for a year. ... Felipe met some North American Christians who told us about an underground movement that had been helping Central American refugees cross into the United States. They explained to us that we would have to wade a river from Mexico into Arizona, which we agreed to do. And so a few days later we started on the final leg of our journey. We made it across the border into the southern United States, and from there we were transported to the Vermont monastery where we now live. ...

Slowly we are adapting to our new life. A tutor comes five days a week to teach us English, but we still have many adjustments to make. We're not used to wearing shoes all day, every day, and we still are not accustomed to sleeping past sunrise. And the food here! In our village, we rarely ate hot meals at all, let alone once or twice a day. After years of living on tortillas, our stomachs are now filled with meat and vegetables. ...

We are a working couple. Felipe is clearing land and helping the brothers with the farming, and I give weaving classes to the women from town. Eventually, we would like to become independent enough to be able to settle in the community on our own.

Of course, that will be very difficult, because we are considered illegal aliens and cannot get working papers. Also, for at least a while longer, we must wear scarves on our faces whenever strangers are around; we're still trying to conceal our identities in case the Guatemalan army is looking for us or wishes to take revenge on the relatives we left behind. ...

We hope to return to Guatemala someday, but we realize we may have a long time to wait. In the meantime, we are thankful to be alive. We are looking for a sign from God that we can live peacefully and safely in the land where my people have lived for thousands of years. Until then, we are pilgrims.

"We Fled for Our Lives," by Elena Ixcot as told to Sara Nelson, *Redbook*, November, 1984.

We Change — Traditions Remain

Traditions, whether music for the ear, food for the body, or stories for the soul, are called folkways. Folkways are important expressions of every culture and nation. Folkways keep heritage and history alive. They are bridges from one generation to the next. For immigrants, folkways are bridges to their homeland; links to the memories, people, and traditions of the past. Folkways carry on the traditions of a people from one generation to the next.

The art, storytelling, music, dance, and foods of Mexico and Central America are a fascinating combination of Indian, Spanish, and American influences. Under Spanish dominion, Indian heritage was discouraged or destroyed. Catholicism became the dominant religion. Spanish rulers kept natives poor, uneducated, and in what amounted to economic slavery. In the early 1800s, Spanish control in Central America ended in country after country. However, the struggle for true freedom was just beginning. War, dictatorships, and poverty combined to make life very hard for most of the people living in Central America and Mexico. A few people owned most of the land. Farmers struggled to feed their families and paid terribly high rents for property. The governments in power seemed to care little for those without property. In Nicaragua, for example, 25 percent of the landowners owned 80 percent of all the property in the country in 1970. The rest of the people struggled to survive with little or no government help.

How does this history affect traditions and folkways? Some Indian folkways have disappeared. And many Central Americans express themselves creatively, but in practical ways. For example, women may spend their time weaving cloth, making clothes, and painting ceramic pots. Life is hard, and artistic expression must fit into the hard work necessary to get food, clothing, and shelter.

Central America struggles with ongoing political conflict. In some Central American countries, mural painting has become a way to express political opinions and creativity at the same time. In Nicaragua and El Salvador, especially, poetry and literature are often focused around political themes. Again, artistic expression adapts to the concerns of daily survival.

In Mexico and Central America, the holidays, art, and traditions of the Catholic Church cannot be separated from the folkways of the country. Most fiestas or festivals are linked with Catholic holidays. Painting and literature often have religious themes as well.

Incan, Mayan, and Aztec traditions influence the Indian cultures, especially in Guatemala and Mexico. Ancient images of the sun, mountains, snakes, and corn are found in weaving and painting.

Mexican and Central American immigrants in the United States treasure their fiestas and holidays. Cinco de Mayo festivities and 15th birthday celebrations for girls are occasions for extravagant celebration. The smell of plaintains cooking or tortillas frying means more than a good meal. It is a link between the old and the new — between the homeland and the new home.

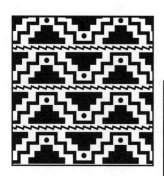

Folkways in a Nation of Immigrants

The following projects will help you learn about the traditions and folkways of Mexican and Central American immigrants. Learning and enjoying the art, food, stories, music, drama, and crafts of other cultures is like opening a window into the history and heritage of other people. You will experience traditions still practiced in Mexico and Central America today. And you will learn to appreciate traditions practiced by your neighbors and fellow Americans.

❦ Prepare the recipe for baked plaintains found in this section. Or find a different recipe from Mexico or another Central American country. Find out about the food and any traditions that go with it. Share the food with your class, and tell the class what you've learned.

❦ Your teacher has instructions for making a Mexican "yarn painting." Follow these instructions to make a picture of your own.

❦ Murals are common in Mexico, Nicaragua, and El Salvador. Often, murals have political themes, showing people voting, working their own land, or just living in peace. Find examples of the clothing and housing common to one of these countries. Look at pictures of people from the country you've chosen, then design and paint a mural depicting people or places in this country on large sheets of paper. If you find examples of artwork from that culture, try to paint in the same style. Acrylics, watercolors, or tempera paints work well.

❦ Guatemalan fabric is famous for its beautiful colors and textures. Women in Guatemala today weave using "backstrap" or "belt" looms designed by ancient Mayan weavers many centuries ago. Take a photo trip to area import and fabric stores where woven fabric from Guatemala is sold. With the shop owner's permission, take photos of Guatemalan cloth, focusing on the different patterns and colors commonly used in Guatemalan fabric. You might also find and photograph other interesting items like purses, wall hangings, or belts.

❦ Salvadoran poets Manlio Argueta and Roque Dalton were political activists as well as poets. Find out as much as you can about these two artists. Give an oral report to your class, and include a poem written by one of them.

❦ In Guatemala, children and adults alike love shadow puppets. Guatemalan shadow puppets are very similar to those used in China and Japan, on the other side of the world. Guatemalan shadow puppets are moved with sticks instead of strings. Find a Guatemalan or Central American folktale. Find instructions for making shadow puppets and design puppets for use with this story. Using a chair, sheet, and reading lamp, you can construct a theater for your puppets. Perform the folktale with your puppets for a younger class.

❦ Find out about Nicaraguan poets Ernesto Cardenal and Rubén Darío. Read examples of their poetry to your class and tell about their lives. Like their counterparts in El Salvador, Cardenal and Darío are very political in their writing.

❦ Nicaraguans have made macramé for centuries. The poorest people knot beautiful hammocks for sleeping and string bags for carrying food. Learn some macramé knots and make a plant hanger, wall hanging, or string bag

Folkways in a Nation of Immigrants

☙ Make a piñata in the traditional Mexican manner. Star and animal shapes are common. Find out what colors are most often used. If you fill your creation with candy or small gifts, your class could have a taste of Mexico with a piñata party.

☙ Find a traditional folktale from Mexico or any Central American country. Folktales are always told orally, so learn it well enough to tell it in front of your class.

☙ The sun is a common theme in Mexican artwork. Find photos or drawings of some examples. Using clay, paint, string, or folded paper, duplicate a traditional sun-figure plaque.

☙ Find out how people from one of the countries studied here celebrate holidays. In El Salvador, the Procession of the Palm Leaves is a special holiday. Mexicans celebrate Cinco de Mayo to mark their independence day. Every country celebrates Christmas and other religious holidays in unique ways. Choose one country to learn about and tell your class about its holiday traditions. If possible, recreate one of these traditions for the class.

Platanos al Horno (Baked Plantains)

INGREDIENTS

2 tablespoons sugar

1 teaspoon ground cinnamon

2 ripe plantains, with black skins

2 tablespoons butter

1. Mix sugar and cinnamon together.

2. Peel the plantains and split them open lengthwise, but do not cut completely through.

3. Sprinkle them inside and out with the sugar mixture.

4. Cut dabs of butter into the slits.

5. Coat a baking dish with butter and place the plantains in the dish.

6. Bake at 350 degrees for 20 to 30 minutes, until soft and brown.

Serve warm with fresh cream and honey.

Folkways in a Nation of Immigrants

The Indian people of western Mexico often tell the stories and myths of their culture with "paintings" made of yarn. The pictures here show one example of a yarn painting. Now you can do your own yarn painting and tell your own story.

MATERIALS NEEDED:

pencil or marker

heavy cardboard

yarn scraps

white glue

scissors

Mexican Yarn Painting

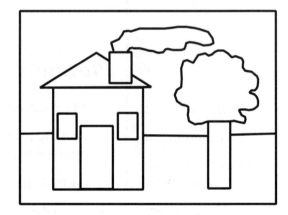

1. With a pencil or marker, draw a picture in outline form on the cardboard, like the picture at right. Your picture should show a scene from a story you want to tell.

2. Spread glue, a small area at a time. You don't want the glue to dry before you put the yarn on the painting.

3. Using different colored yarn, fill in each shape by pressing yarn onto the glue. Start on the outside edge of each shape. Fill in the whole picture with yarn. (See the example of a filled-in picture above.)

4. Let dry thoroughly.

Research & Writing Topics

The following list includes suggestions for individual or group research and writing projects for this unit on immigrants from Mexico and Central America.

❦ Read a fiction book about the life of Mexican immigrants or Central American refugees in America. Write a report telling the class about the story and what it means to you.

❦ Trace a large map of Mexico and Central America. Using magazines, photocopied pictures from library and reference books, and on-line graphics, find pictures of as many cultural/ethnic groups in the region as possible. Look especially for illustrations of national costumes, traditions, or lifestyles. Attach pictures to show where people live. Write captions under your photos giving information about each ethnic group, its people, traditions, and unique ways.

❦ Many people from Mexico and Central America have entered and continue to enter the United States illegally. Sometimes this practice is called *bajo alambre,* or "beneath the barbed wire." Find out why people come to the U.S. this way. Why do some U.S. citizens think this is bad for our country? How do the many thousands of illegal immigrants affect the U.S.? Do they help the economy of our nation, or harm it? How? Find out about issues like the use of public education, welfare, medical care, and employment. Write a report telling what questions and problems are connected to illegal immigration. Be sure to give your own opinions about how the United States government could solve these problems.

❦ What is NAFTA? What is its purpose? Why did the U.S., Canada, and Mexico make this agreement? Do you think the agreement has worked? How do you think NAFTA might affect illegal immigration to the U.S.?

❦ In the late 1980s, the U.S. government decided that some illegal immigrants could apply for amnesty. Find out what this means. Find out more about the program and how it worked. Contact the U.S. Immigration and Naturalization Service office in your area to ask about the amnesty program. Write a report about what you learn.

❦ If you live in an area where Mexican immigrants have settled, contact a local Mexican American social services agency or social organization. Interview someone who settled in the U.S. Find out why that person left Mexico and what he or she thinks of the U.S. Write a report about what you learn to share with your class.

❦ Find out about the ancient history of Mexico. Learn about the Olmecs, Maya, and Aztecs. Who were they? Where did they live? What was unique about their cultures? Find out about these ancestors of people living in Mexico and Central America today.

Research & Writing Topics

Mexico and Central America

❦ Spanish explorers claimed the areas now known as Mexico and most of Central America as colonies of Spain during the 16th century. Choose one country and find out what happened during the period of Spanish colonization. How did Spain colonize the country? Why was the country colonized in the first place? How did this country win its freedom? How did Spanish culture influence the culture of this country?

❦ In 1983, 43 percent of all Mexican citizens were under 14 years of age. How do you think the large number of young people affects the Mexican economy? Look at issues of jobs, family life, and migration to other countries, especially the U.S.

❦ Learn about migrant workers in the United States. Here are some words, names, and topics to include in your report:
> Cesar Chavez, green card, United Farm Workers Union, Immigration and Naturalization Service, boycotts during the 1970s, "wetbacks," "coyotes."

In the past, most migrant workers in this country were Mexican. Is that still true today?

❦ Learn about the civil war in El Salvador. What parties were involved? How was the U.S. involved? Here are some topics and words to learn about for your report:
> FMLN, scorched earth policy, depopulation, death squads, Mesa Grande Refugee camp, "Patria libre o morir" ("A free country or death"), liberation theology, Oscar Romero, The Central American Peace Accord of 1987

❦ What is the Basic Law of Land Reform? Why is it important in El Salvador's history? Learn how land ownership shaped El Salvador's political history. How did the land reform issue affect immigration? How did it affect the civil war? Write a report about what you learn.

❦ Research the life of either Oscar Romero or Jean Donovan, two well-known people who died during El Salvador's civil war. Although they were only two of many thousands of people who died, their stories are of particular interest. Write a report about what you learn.

❦ Learn about the Overground Railroad and the sanctuary movement, which were active in the 1980s. Why were people, organizations, and churches in the United States involved in finding sanctuary for Salvadoran, Nicaraguan, and Guatemalan refugees? Call area groups, such as churches, Catholic Worker cooperatives, World Relief, church denominational offices, or refugee service organizations to find people who were involved in these movements. What happened and why did they participate? Write a report about what you learn.

Research & Writing Topics

**Mexico and
Central America**

🐦 Learn about the history of Nicaragua. Here are some words, names, and topics to assist you:

> Spanish rule, Augusto Cesar Sandino, the Somoza family, Sandinistas, Contras, United States funding of Contras, Sandinista Socialist movement, Daniel Ortega.

Describe how this history affected emigration from Nicaragua to the U.S. Write a report about what you learn.

🐦 Guatemala's history is similar to that of other countries in Central America. After Spanish control ended, the next century was marked by a series of military dictatorships, revolts, coups, and elections that we in the U.S. would not recognize as democratic. Learn about Guatemala's history. Here are some names to find out about:

> Jorge Ubico, Guerrilla Army of the Poor, Jorge Serrano, Ramiro de Leon.

Find out about the role of land ownership in Guatemala's history of revolution, guerrilla warfare, and violence. Think about how this history might have affected immigration to the U.S. Write a report about what you learn.

Resource List

General

Books:

Katz, William Loren, *A History of Multicultural America: The Great Migrations 1880s-1912*. Austin, Tex.: Raintree Steck-Vaughn, 1993.

Loescher, Gil and Ann Dull, *The World's Refugees: A Test of Humanity*. San Diego: Harcourt Brace Jovanovich, 1982.

Video:

The Golden Door: Our Nation of Immigrants. Knowledge Unlimited, 1996. (An overview of the history of immigration in America.)

Posters:

America: A Nation of Immigrants, Knowledge Unlimited, 1996. (Eight poster set.)

East Asia

Books:

Chan, Sucheng, *Asian Americans: An Interpretive History*. Boston: Twayne, 1991.

Hong, Maria, ed., *Growing Up Asian American*. New York: William Morrow, 1993.

Lehrer, Brian, *The Peoples of North America: The Korean Americans*. New York: Chelsea House, 1988.

Melendy, Howard Brett, *Asians in America: Filipinos, Koreans, and East Indians*. Boston: Twayne, 1977.

Patterson, Wayne and Hyung-chan Kim, *The Koreans in America*. Minneapolis: Lerner, 1977.

Perrin, Linda, *Coming to America: Immigrants from the Far East*. New York: Delacorte, 1980.

Steiner, Stan, *Fusang: The Chinese Who Built America*. New York: Harper & Row, 1979.

Takaki, Ronald, *A Different Mirror: A History of Multicultural America*. Boston: Little, Brown and Company, 1993.

Wilson, Robert Arden, and Bill Hosokawa, *East to America: A History of the Japanese in the United States*. New York: William Morrow, 1980.

Yep, Laurence, *Dragonwings*. New York: Harper & Row, 1975.

Yep, Laurence, *Sea Glass*. New York: Harper & Row, 1979.

Yep, Laurence, *Thief of Hearts*. New York: HarperCollins, 1995.

Southeast Asia

Books:

Auerbach, Susan, *American Voices: Vietnamese Americans*. Vero Beach, Fla.: Rourke Corporation, 1991.

Bandon, Alexandra, *Footsteps to America: Filipino Americans*. New York: New Discovery Books, 1993.

Resource List

Cha, Dia, *Dia's Story Cloth: The Hmong People's Journey of Freedom*. New York: Lee & Low Books, 1996.

Fields, Rick and Don Farber, *Taking Refuge in L.A.: Life in a Vietnamese Buddhist Temple*. New York: Aperture Foundation, 1987.

Greenblatt, Miriam, *Cambodia: Enchantment of the World*. Chicago: Children's Press, 1995.

Library of Nations: Southeast Asia. New York: Prentice Hall, 1987.

McNair, Sylvia, *Thailand: Enchantment of the World*. Chicago: Children's Press, 1987.

Melendy, Howard Brett, *Asians in America: Filipinos, Koreans, and East Indians*. Boston: Twayne, 1977.

Rutledge, Paul, *The Vietnamese in America*. Minneapolis: Lerner, 1987.

St. Pierre, Stephanie, ed., *Teenage Refugees from Cambodia Speak Out*. New York: Rosen Publishing Group, 1995.

Schmidt, Jeremy and Ted Wood, *Two Lands, One Heart: An American Boy's Journey to His Mother's Vietnam*. New York: Walker and Co., 1995.

Whelan, Gloria, *Goodbye, Vietnam*. New York: Alfred Knopf, 1992.

Wright, David, *Vietnam: Enchantment of the World*. Chicago: Children's Press, 1989.

Magazine Articles

National Geographic articles include:

June 1987, "Laos"

October 1988, "The Hmong in America"

January 1990, "Nest Gatherers of Tiger Cave"

April 1991, "The World's Food Supply at Risk"

February 1993, "The Mekong: A Haunted River's Season of Peace"

May 1994, "Rice: The Essential Harvest"

April 1995, "The New Saigon"

South Asia and the Middle East

Books:

Alexander, Lloyd, *The Jedera Adventure*. New York: Dutton Books, 1989.

Ashabranner, Brent, *An Ancient Heritage: The Arab-American Minority*. New York: HarperCollins, 1991.

Bagai, Leona B., *The East Indians and the Pakistanis in America*. Minneapolis: Lerner, 1967.

Courlander, Harold, *The Tiger's Whisker*. New York: Henry Holt, 1995. (A collection of folktales.)

Harick, Elsa Marston, *The Lebanese in America*. Minneapolis: Lerner, 1987.

Jaffrey, Madhur, *Seasons of Splendor: Indian Folklore*, New York: Puffin, 1987.

Jordan, Ruth, *Daughter of the Waves*. New York: Taplinger, 1983. (A story of pre-war Palestine.)

Resource List

L'Engle, Madeleine, *The Glorious Impossible*. New York: Simon and Schuster, 1990.

Long, Cathryn J., *The Middle East in Search of Peace*. Brookfield, Conn.: Millbrook Press, 1994.

McCaughrean, Geraldine (retold), *One Thousand and One Arabian Nights*. New York: Oxford University Press, 1982.

Melendy, Howard Brett, *Asians in America: Filipinos, Koreans, and East Indians*. Boston: Twayne, 1977.

Naff, Alixa, *Becoming American: The Early Arab Immigrant Experience*. Carbondale, Ill.: Southern Illinois University Press, 1985.

Najib Mahfuz, *The Journey of Ibn Fattouma*. New York: Doubleday, 1992.

Salzman, M., *War and Peace in the Persian Gulf: What Teenagers Want to Know*. Princeton, N.J.: Peterson's Guides, 1991. (Interviews with teenagers from the Middle East.)

Temple, Frances, *The Bedouins' Gazelle*. New York: Orchard Press, 1996.

Eastern Europe

Books:

Ackerman, Karen, *The Night Crossing*. New York: Alfred A. Knopf, 1994.

Angell, Judie, *One-Way to Ansonia*. New York: Bradbury Press, 1985. (Polish-Jewish experience in America.)

Feder, Paula, *The Feather-Bed Journey*. Niles, Ill.: Albert Whitman, 1995. (Polish Jews)

Fisher, Leonard, *A Russian Farewell*. New York: Four Winds Press, 1995.

Gray, Bettyanne, *Manya's Story*. Minneapolis: Lerner, 1978. (Ukraine)

Grocza, Rezcoe, *The Hungarians in America*. Minneapolis: Lerner, 1969.

Holman, Felice, *The Wild Children*. New York: Puffin, 1985. (Story of orphaned children after the Russian Revolution.)

Kelly, Eric, *The Trumpeter of Krakow*. New York: Aladdin Books, 1992.

Magocsi, Paul R., *The Peoples of North America: The Russian Americans*. New York: Chelsea House, 1989.

Moscinski, Sharon, *Tracing Our Polish Roots*. Santa Fe, N.M.: John Muir Publications, 1994.

Muggamin, Howard, *The Peoples of North America: The Jewish Americans*. New York: Chelsea House, 1988.

Pelloski, Anne, *First Farm in the Valley: Anna's Story*. New York: Philomel Books, 1982. (Polish immigrant story.)

Pelloski, Anne, *Stairstep Farm: Anna Rosa's Story*. New York: Philomel Books, 1981. (Polish immigrant story.)

Pitt, Nancy, *Beyond the High White Wall*. New York: Charles Scribner's Sons, 1986. (Ukraine)

Ross, Lillian Hammer, *Sarah, Also Known as Hannah*. Niles, Ill.: Albert Whitman, 1994. (Story of a Jewish girl from Ukraine. Powerful descriptions of Ellis Island.)

Sagan, Miriam, *Tracing Our Jewish Roots*. Santa Fe, N.M.: John Muir Publications, 1993.

Resource List

Saxon-Ford, Stephanie, *The Peoples of North America: The Czech Americans*. New York: Chelsea House, 1989.

Stolarik, M. Mark, *The Slovak Americans*. New York: Chelsea House, 1988.

Wiesel, Elie, *Night*. New York: Avon, 1969.

Yolen, Jane, *The Devil's Arithmetic*. New York: Viking, 1988.

Film:
Night Crossing. A Disney Family Favorites Film available in libraries and rental outlets. Based upon the true story of a family that escaped from East Germany in a homemade hot air balloon.

Western Europe

Books:
Blumenthal, Shirley, and Jerome S. Ozer, *Coming to America: Immigrants from the British Isles*. New York: Delacorte, 1980.

Cornelius, James M., *The Peoples of North America: The English Americans*. New York: Chelsea House, 1990.

Cornelius, James M., *The Peoples of North America: The Norwegian Americans*. New York: Chelsea House, 1988.

Johnson, James E., *The Scots and Scotch-Irish in America*. Minneapolis: Lerner, 1991.

Jones, Jayne Clark, *The Greeks in America*. Minneapolis: Lerner, 1990.

Morrice, Polly, *The Peoples of North America: The French Americans*. New York: Chelsea House, 1988.

Perl, Lila, *Hunter's Stew and Hangtown Fry: What Pioneer America Ate and Why*. Boston: Houghton Mifflin, 1977.

Robbins, Albert, *Coming to America: Immigrants from Northern Europe*. New York: Delacorte, 1981.

Schouweiler, Thomas, *Germans in America*. Minneapolis: Lerner, 1994.

Shaw, Janet Beeler. *Kirsten Learns a Lesson*. Middleton, Wis.: Pleasant Co., 1986.

Films/Videos:
Films available from Her Own Words; Jocelyn Riley, producer. Riley's collection of documentary films are particularly appropriate for unit studies on Western European immigration. The following films are pertinent:

America Fever, 1994.

Dane County/Wisconsin Pioneer Women's Diaries, 1986.

Patchwork: A Kaleidoscope of Quilts, 1989.

Prairie Cabin: A Norwegian Pioneer Woman's Story, 1991.

Films may be available through regional libraries or educational resource centers. Information about these excellent films is available from Her Own Words, P.O. Box 5264, Madison, Wisconsin 53705, (608)271-7083.

Resource List

Heartland, 1979. A well-produced film available on video about the life of Elinor Pruitt Stewart, a homesteader in Montana. Authentic and age-appropriate.

Africa

Books:

Altman, Susan, *Extraordinary Black Americans.* Chicago: Children's Press, 1989.

Asante, Molefi Kete, *African American History: A Journey of Liberation.* Maywood, N.J.: The Peoples Publishing Group, 1995.

Brodie, James Michael, *Created Equal: The Lives and Ideas of Black American Innovators.* New York: William Morrow, 1993.

Curry, Barbara K. and James Michael Brodie, *Sweet Words So Brave: The Story of African American Literature.* Madison, Wis.: Zino Press Children's Books, 1996. (Provides an overview of African American literature from slave days to the present.)

Hughes, Langston, Milton Meltzer, and C. Eric Lincoln, *A Pictorial History of Black Americans.* New York: Crown, 1968.

Jacobs, Harriet, *Incidents in the Life of a Slave Girl.* New York: Oxford University Press, 1988. (An intense, sometimes disturbing story for advanced readers. Interlibrary loan suggested.)

Johnston, Brenda, *Between the Devil and the Sea; the Life of James Forten.* San Diego: Harcourt, Brace, Jovanovich, 1974.

Katz, William, *Breaking the Chains: African American Slave Resistance.* New York: Atheneum, 1990.

Knight, Michael, *In Chains to Louisiana: Solomon Northrup's Story.* Hauppauge, N.Y.: Barrons, 1971.

Lester, Julius, *To Be a Slave.* New York: Dial, 1968.

Northrup, David, ed., *The Atlantic Slave Trade.* Lexington, Mass.: D.C. Heath and Company, 1994.

Smead, Howard, *The Peoples of North American: The Afro-Americans.* New York: Chelsea House, 1989.

Stanley, Leotha, *Be A Friend: the Story of African American Music in Song, Words and Pictures.* Madison, Wis.: Zino Press Children's Books, 1994. (A music tape comes with this book.)

Taulbert, Clifton, *When We Were Colored.* New York: Penguin, 1995. (One man's account of growing up in the segregated South.)

Taulbert, Clifton, *The Last Train North.* New York: Penguin, 1995. (The sequel to *When We Were Colored,* as the author moved north.)

Warner, Lucille, *From Slave to Abolitionist: The Life of William Wells Brown.* New York: Dial, 1976.

White, Anne, *North to Liberty: The Story of the Underground Railroad* . Champaign, Ill.: Garrard, 1972.